CW01024568

KEYS TO TRANSFORMATION

Ceri Richards and Dylan Thomas

KEYS TO TRANSFORMATION

A Monograph by

RICHARD BURNS

LONDON
THE ENITHARMON PRESS
1981

First published in 1981
by the Enitharmon Press
22 Huntingdon Road
East Finchley
London N2 9DU

©Richard Burns 1981

Drawings and paintings by Ceri Richards © Frances Richards
and the Trustees of the Estate of the late Ceri Richards

Poems by Dylan Thomas © J. M. Dent and Son

ISBN 0 905289 08 0 (wrappers)
ISBN 0 905289 13 7 (hardbound)

The Enitharmon Press acknowledges
financial assistance from
the Arts Council of Great Britain

*Printed and made in Great Britain by
Skelton's Press, Castle Street, Wellingborough, Northamptonshire.*

For Kim Landers, Jean Markale and Roberto Sanesi
and in memory of Carl Gustav Jung

ACKNOWLEDGEMENTS

Poems by Dylan Thomas are reproduced with the permission of J. M. Dent and Sons Ltd. The plates are reproduced with the permission of Mrs. Frances Richards, Mrs. Rachel Patterson, and Mrs. Rhiannon Gooding (as Trustees of the Estate of the late Ceri Richards), Mrs. Esther Thomas, Swansea Central Library and the Tate Gallery. C. G. Jung's letter to Ceri Richards and other quotations from Jung's writings are reproduced with the permission of Routledge and Kegan Paul Ltd.

Of the many people who have helped me in writing this monograph, I should particularly like to thank all the members of Ceri Richards's family for their information, friendship and constant advice and encouragement: above all, Mrs. Frances Richards (the artist's widow) and Mrs. Rachel Patterson (his elder daughter) and her husband Colin. For additional information, my thanks also to Mrs. Esther Thomas (the artist's sister), Mrs. Rhiannon Gooding and her husband Mel, Mrs. Gwen Watkins, the Hon. Mrs. Lucille Frost, Mr. J. A. Davies, the Swansea County Librarian, and, for providing me with the full text of Ceri Richards's letter to C. G. Jung, Dr. Gerhard Adler, the editor of Jung's *Letters*. For invaluable criticism, I should like to thank Kim Landers, Rachel Patterson and Walter Perrie; and for their suggestions and, even more important to me, their moral support, Alan Clodd (Enitharmon Press), Alan and Jean Denman, John Paul Dick, Diana May, Harry Stamper and John Wilson. All defects and errors are my own. Finally, I am grateful to the Arts Council of Great Britain for the fellowship in creative writing at the Victoria Centre for Adult Education, Gravesend, Kent (1979-81), which provided me with financial security and time to write.

R.B.

CONTENTS

The language of dream, with its unlimited lexicon of image, situation, gesture and utterance, is capable of a discourse continually multivalent, fluid and ambiguous. It relates to our experience in a quite different way than do the languages of the sciences, logic and reportage. The latter seek to avoid ambiguity and to operate within the limits of the highly restricted functional aims of their respective language games. Myth and some kinds of poetry use language in such a way that it partakes of some of the characteristics of dream-language and of science-language.

In the interpretation of a dream, a particular image or utterance may be understood as sustaining at one and the same time mutually exclusive interpretations. As in the dream, so in life. A named object, like a dream, subsists within a vastly complex web of relations. The languages of science attempt to cope with this complexity by piecemeal description. Having had their lexical elements selected in part on the basis of the exclusion of ambiguity, they are, outwith their own spheres of application, inadequate to the expression of those elements in our experience which we do find ambiguous. It is in precisely this area that art excels.

WALTER PERRIE

It is equally a grave mistake to think that it is enough to gain some understanding of the images and that knowledge can here make a halt. Insight into them must be converted into an ethical obligation. Not to do so is to fall prey to the power principle, and this produces dangerous effects which are destructive not only to others but also to the knower. The images of the unconscious place a great responsibility upon a man. Failure to understand them, or a shirking of ethical responsibility, deprives him of his wholeness and imposes a painful fragmentariness on his life.

C. G. JUNG

ABBREVIATIONS

DPDT: Ceri Richards, *Drawings to Poems by Dylan Thomas*, Enitharmon Press, London, 1980.

CP: Dylan Thomas, *Collected Poems 1934-1952*, J. M. Dent, London, 1952.

GWCR: Roberto Sanesi (ed.), *The Graphic Works of Ceri Richards*, Gino Cerastico, Milan, 1973.

A Retrospective Introduction

In Autumn 1976, I paid several visits to Frances Richards at her new home in Barnes, as we had decided to work on a book together – of her drawings and my poems. During one of these visits, she told me she had something 'very special' to show me, and handed me a copy of Dylan Thomas's *Collected Poems 1934-1952*.[1] I was already familiar with a number of the paintings and lithographs which her late husband, Ceri Richards, had based on Thomas's work. I had also known Thomas's poems well since my teens, when my enthusiasm for them had been enormous, although by now I felt I had outgrown them. For this reason I was not prepared for the effect on me of what followed.

Nearly a third of the pages in the book were covered in drawings by Ceri Richards. Frances Richards told me that they had all been composed in the space of twenty-four hours in their house in Edith Grove, Chelsea, only one day before Dylan Thomas died in New York. The first one that struck me was a racy, affectionate sketch on the title page, of a figure on a balcony looking out over a bay, representing Thomas at his house in Laugharne. On the dedication page, alongside the words 'To Caitlin', was a simple line-drawing, from memory, of the poet's wife, also looking out to sea with clouds and hills behind. The first page of the 'Author's Prologue' was adorned with a pair of hands, one resting on a knee, and the other busily scribbling away at a page on the corner of a table, with flowers tumbling from pen and text. The drawings, in indian ink, were so fresh it seemed they had only just dried. They wound, wrapped and insinuated themselves among the poems, incorporating the words into new visual patterns of their own. Interested, I flicked through all of them in a few minutes, wanting to take in an overall impression as quickly as possible. By the time I had finished, interest had turned to excitement. Quite apart from the apparently effortless and spontaneous quality of the drawings, it was clear that Ceri Richards had responded to Thomas's poems in an intensely personal and unique way; and in the context of Frances Richards's comments about the date when the drawings were composed, I was particularly fascinated by the presence of death which loomed eerily in several of them, in the repeated motif of skulls. I knew I was handling something unusual, even extraordinary, which ought to be published. I telephoned Alan Clodd, the editor of Enitharmon Press, who was due to bring out the poems and drawings which Frances Richards and I were working on,[2] and urged him to see the book and to consider it, subject to his obtaining rights to reprint Thomas's poems. I offered to help in whatever way I could, and to write a preface.

The book was published by Enitharmon Press in 1980, with the title *Ceri Richards, Drawings to Poems by Dylan Thomas* (henceforward referred to by the abbreviation *DPDT*).[3] This monograph is intended primarily as a companion to that book, and as a commentary on it. It is also, I hope, several other things besides.

In the two years that followed, I pieced together more information about the drawings – from Frances Richards herself, from leads she had given me, and from hunches of my own. I found out that it was one of four copies of Thomas's *Collected Poems* which Richards had made drawings in, all around the same period (November 1953) when Dylan Thomas died. The second of these variants, I learned from Frances Richards, was owned by Mrs. Esther Thomas, Ceri's sister (but no relation of Dylan's). Then, remembering a brief hint in the study of Ceri Richards's graphics by the Italian poet and critic Roberto Sanesi, which I had translated six years previously,[4] I traced a third variant to the reserve collection in Swansea Central Library, discovering that it had been purchased by them from Richards in March 1954. The fourth variant, which Frances Richards believed was owned by the Hon. Mrs. Lucille Frost, an ex-patient of Carl Gustav Jung's, and a friend of Ceri Richards and admirer of his work, I was unable to trace despite a long drawn-out correspondence with Mrs. Frost, who was now a very old lady, and her family, in Portugal.[5] But although this line of enquiry proved disappointing in itself, it led to another which, to me, was exciting. Frances Richards told me that the drawings in *DPDT* which accompanied the poem 'I dreamed my genesis' (reproduced on the front cover of this edition) was one of a series of three works by her husband with the obscure title *Afal du Brogŵyr* ('Black Apple of Gower'). I had been more struck by this particular drawing than by any of the others in the book when

I had first seen it: it stood out not only for its wealth of detail and the amount of attention Richards had devoted to it, but for its puzzling and mysterious content, for which it was clear at first glance that a separate symbolic or allegorical key was needed, whereas most of the other drawings could be read more easily by direct reference to the imagery and themes of the poems they accompanied.

The other two works in the *Afal du Brogŵyr* series were an oil-painting (fig. 39), owned by Mrs. Rachel Patterson (the elder daughter of Ceri and Frances) and her husband Colin, and an earlier study in chalk and water-colour on paper rubbed over wood (fig. 36), which the same Mrs. Lucille Frost who owned the untraced variant of the *Collected Poems* had bought from Ceri Richards and given to Jung as a personal present. Even more interestingly, Jung had written a letter to Richards about this painting, which was reprinted in volume 2 of his *Letters*, together with a black and white photograph of it and a note which incorporated some remarks made by Richards to Dr. Gerhard Adler, the editor of the volume, about the work.[6] The tone and content of Jung's letter, which focused on the painting's symbolism, seemed as mysterious as the drawing in the book itself, and made it clear that he had seen unusual depths of meaning in it. In the context of my own separate interest in Jung's writings, I found all this intriguing, and began to think more deeply about the patterns of imagery running through the drawings in the book, as well as in the three works in the *Afal du Brogŵyr* series, and even went so far as to make detailed charts of their recurrent motifs. In September 1978, I wrote to Gerhard Adler and asked if he could send me a copy of Richards's letter to him about the water-colour study. He wrote back apologetically, saying that he could not find it. Then, unexpectedly, in November 1980, when I had already completed the first draft of this monograph, he wrote again, saying that he had managed to trace it, and enclosing the original letter.

By Autumn 1979, I had gathered all the relevant information which I thought I was ever likely to receive, and set to work on my preface to the book. What was required was a couple of thousand words, no more, presenting the material to the reader in a moderately informed but general way. But by now I had far too many facts to use, most of which were unlikely to interest the casual reader or art-lover, as well as a host of half-formed questions and connections in my own mind arising out of the material, but not always related directly to it, which I wanted to pursue.

Without realising it, I had become deeply involved, and not just intellectually. Emotions, intuitions and even physical sensations, as well as 'rational' ideas, were being triggered in me by the material, and the need to clarify and express them was growing into a personal commitment to integrate and understand transformations which by then were actively happening inside myself at least partially as a result of contact with Richards's work. My preface grew and grew – five, ten, twenty thousand words, and more. When I finally presented it to the publisher three months later, it was clearly both too long and inappropriate: clearly, that is, to everybody except myself, since I had now become totally immersed in the material. He asked me to extract and adapt the first part of my essay, which would serve as an adequate introduction to the drawings, and suggested I rewrite the rest, which he offered to publish separately.

All this had started off modestly enough. It had seemed important to me to document the order of composition of the three known variants of the book as accurately as I could. This led me naturally to asking which, if any, of the variants could be considered the final version, and also to thinking about Richards's compositional method: how he would gradually transform a mental image, impression or idea, through a series of sketches, into a finished artefact. Then, brooding over the relationship between the poems and drawings for them, and also over Jung's comments on the *Afal du Brogŵyr*, I began to ask questions about a whole range of related issues. First, I became interested in Thomas's influence on the entire development of Richards's work, which meant the very large number of paintings, drawings and lithographs which were derived from lines or images of Thomas's, from 1945 when he first illustrated 'The force that through the green fuse drives the flower' for *Poetry London* (figs. 40-42), until his death in 1971. Gradually realising how pervasive and far-reaching this influence was, I found myself having to stop short of attempting anything like a complete cataloguing or analysis of these works, since this was clearly outside my scope and would diffuse my focus from *DPDT* and the *Afal du Brogŵyr*, which were what I was primarily interested in. A systematic study of this kind, however, is certainly called for, and I hope that some of what follows may spur another writer to take it up. All the same, I did explore a sufficient number of Richards's other works relating to Dylan Thomas to see coherent patterns of symbolism emerging, which I thought corres- ponded to – and revealed – an inner psychic development in the artist, in the

16

same manner as a Jungian interpretation reveals the inner connectedness in a sequence of dreams. All of this sent me back to the *Afal du Brogŵyr* series, as the most important key to unlock this development. For this reason, much of this monograph is taken up with discussion of this series, and presents arguments for considering the *Afal du Brogŵyr* oil-painting as one of the finest of Richards's works, and also (following Jung) as among the most profound and mysterious of our time.

Correspondingly, I also thought more about the insights into Thomas's poems which Richards's readings of them offered, many of which I believed were both strikingly original, qualitatively different from the reams of literary criticism, biography, memoirs and gossip published about Thomas, and probably more interesting and useful than any of them: views which I still hold. This in turn sent me back again to closer readings of many poems which I believed I had clearly understood long before but which I now found new meanings in, not to mention renewed enjoyment; and this in turn directed me to look more closely at the details in some of Richards's later drawings and lithographs which explored themes from Thomas, particularly those which incorporated scraps of writing in Richards's often almost illegible scrawl. In the reproductions I had of several of these, important details were blurred, because they were either too small or of poor photographic quality; so I visited Rachel and Colin Patterson's house where I was able to see some of the originals, jot down lines and phrases (some of them in mirror-writing), and trace several of these to their sources in poems by Thomas. I also discovered some lettering which quoted the first line of 'The force that through the green fuse drives the flower' scratched into the paint of the large *Afal du Brogŵyr* oil-painting which nobody seemed to have noticed before. All this was exciting and seemed to bear out my interpretations of the *DPDT* series. Even more important to me personally, the emotional impact of the *Afal du Brogŵyr* painting on me (which, previously, I had never looked at very closely) was unlike anything I had experienced from any visual work of art before or have ever experienced since. The large room in the Pattersons' house, which was hung with other canvases by Richards, began to reel around me: I felt dizzy, had to sit down, and found myself weeping. The painting's effect on me was entirely spontaneous and unexpected: whatever was already going on inside me, it connected with at a deep level. I mention this here because it is the clearest indication I can give of the *power* of this work, which no amount of intellectual discussion of its sources, symbolism and so on can ever quite convey adequately.

As for the book itself, I also spent a lot of time thinking about the similarities of Thomas's and Richards's Welsh backgrounds, and the curious correspondences and coincidences relating the dates of composition of *DPDT*, and of Thomas's and Richards's deaths, with patterns of imagery in the work of both of them, and with similar motifs in Celtic myth and literature. Without at least attempting to explore these configurations, I knew that I would be unlikely to account at all adequately for the power I sensed being released through the *DPDT* series and the *Afal du Brogŵyr* oil-painting. The patterns I have traced in this way are inevitably of my own selection, but I have not imposed these arbitrarily upon the material and they can easily be checked against it. I have also deliberately stopped short of making any general claims about the significance of these 'coincidences and correspondences', preferring to let the material speak for itself and the reader make up his or her own mind, since the phenomenon of 'meaningful coincidence' raises very wide philosophical issues which are outside the proper scope of this essay and I could not have hoped to confront them adequately here.[7]

However, the study of symbol-formation and symbol-configurations in the work of a poet or artist, as in myths and dreams, necessarily involves exploration of subjective experience. During Autumn and Winter 1979, when I was working most intensely on patterns of symbolism, I too was beset by a number of strange and even alarming coincidences in my personal life, which seemed to me at the time – and still seem – to be meaningfully related to the material by Richards and Thomas which I was exploring. Jung describes episodes of this kind in his autobiography.[8] It was almost as though the symbols had jumped off the page and were leading separate lives among the events happening around me. All this convinced me even more strongly that art and poetry, like myth, are concerned neither with the mere prettification or decoration of isolated experiences, nor with subjective confession, nor with imitating a 'reality' conceived of as discrete and pre-ordained, but with the constant reorganisation and transformation of the single reality of which they themselves are parts, which is itself in constant process of reorganisation and transformation. As Richards himself wrote: "One can generally say that all artists – poets, musicians, painters, are creating in their own idioms, metaphors for the nature of existence, for

18

the secrets of our time. We are all moved by the beauty and revelation in their utterances – we notice the direction and beauty of the paths they indicate for us, and move towards them.'"[9] Nor, I realised, can symbols in myth, art or poetry be played around or experimented with in the purely 'detached' manner of Western science, any more than, say, 'atomic particles' or 'the stratosphere' (which are themselves also symbols), without their reacting back upon the experimenter in surprising and often alarming ways. The symbols of myth, art and poetry are as deeply engrained into our inner and outer environments as those of science, which in our age most of us are more readily prepared to accept as 'real': like atoms, when fused or split, they too are capable of releasing energies for both good and evil. All of which is to say that symbols in myth, art and poetry should be treated with a respect born of appreciation and understanding of their ecology. The epigraphs of this book, from Walter Perrie[10] and C. G. Jung,[11] have bearings on this complex question.

As for myths, in November 1979, a friend, Alan Denman, lent me a copy of Jean Markale's book, *Women of the Celts*,[12] and I was astonished at both the number, inner cohesion and richness of the Celtic motifs he analysed which were repeated in Richards's work. This was a real find, which could not have been more apt in timing for me: it took me into areas I had not expected to find myself exploring at all when I started writing, although in retrospect it now seems clear that these had been there all along, to be read quite openly, in Thomas's and Richards's work, and only my own ignorance of their sources and blindness to their wider implications had kept them from me.

These areas were sexuality and gender. The patterns which occur in actual relationships between men and women, I saw being mediated through historically determined images and symbols of the opposite sex, with their associated (and equally historically determined) 'values', which we all carry within us. These images and symbols correspond at least in part to the archetypes which Jung called the *anima* (most simply delineated as a male's composite image of femininity) and the *animus* (a female's correspondingly composite image of masculinity). Secondly, working outwards from such images in Richards's and Thomas's work, through Jung, Markale, the *I Ching*,[13] the books of Erich Neumann,[14] and other texts, I began to formulate ideas about the relationship of any artist or poet to his or her own time, and about the social function of art and literature in

19

general. I began to realise the connection between, on the one hand, received symbols of sexuality and gender, with all the subtle balances and oppositions which they permeate through many aspects of our thinking processes and social behaviour, and, on the other, the role of poets and artists, who, by working constantly with such images and symbols, combining them and recombining them, inevitably re-organise and transform their values. The Jungian idea, developed in even more detail by Neumann,[15] that the function of art and literature is to compensate for the consciously held values of the society in which it occurs by constantly drawing attention to values which are repressed or 'kept in shadow', and so, as it were, to ensure that society's psychic health by redressing its one-sidedness, provided insights which tallied well with Markale's analyses of the historical position of women in Celtic societies and of Celtic images of femininity. It began to seem possible to reconcile the idealistic tendencies in Jung and Neumann with Markale's neo-Freudian, pro-Feminist, Marxist approach. My argument then became very simple, and it is roughly as follows: that the key to Richards's and Thomas's works, which unlocks their hidden meaning and also shows why they have impact and importance for our time, is to understand that the principal creative impulse which they shared was celebration of the recessive feminine principle, in defiance of prevailing patterns of contemporary social behaviour which prize masculine qualities at almost all costs. So gradually I discovered, much to my own surprise, that my psychological and symbolistic approach had an implicit historical and social dimension.

One word of warning here, however. I believe it is important to distinguish carefully between the terms 'male' and 'female' on the one hand, and 'masculine' and 'feminine' on the other: as far as these distinctions are concerned, my prime concern in interpreting the patterns and correlations of symbols in human-made artefacts (poems, drawings and paintings) has been with their *gender*; that is, with the traditional patterns of binary thinking which, largely without our realising it, mould and possible even govern language, perceptions and behaviour. I have been dealing then, not directly with real men and women, but with *images* of masculinity and femininity in relation to each other, which are no less real, but of a different order. The *I Ching* shows clearly how through time, words, images and symbols can change either their gender or value or both, quite rapidly and easily. It makes sense to regard transformations of gender among images and symbols as indicators of historical processes and cultural changes which are taking place all the time in both individuals and societies; and that such processes and transformations belong in the real world there can be no doubt. But to confuse 'masculine' with 'male' or 'feminine' with 'female' is to "mistake the map for the territory", which I have been at pains to avoid. One of the main obstacles to a better society is not merely the exploitation of the masses under capitalism, as this is defined in classical Marxist theory, but what Markale calls "the gigantic swindle" which occurs in most so-called 'love-relationships' between men and women in capitalist society. At the centre of this problem, I believe, lies precisely this confusion between sex and gender, which leads to all kinds of misunderstandings, disappointments and tragedies in real human relationships, in and out of marriage, in families, and in bringing up children. This confusion is rooted in prejudices and false expectations, and in not thinking clearly enough about the symbols which influence us at an unconscious or subconscious level. We cannot proceed forward to more humane and intelligent relationships between people unless we try to understand how such prejudices dominate what we think and do; and the latter part of this monograph is, at least in part, an attempt to do this, by stressing that it is a measure of the greatness of artists like Ceri Richards and poets like Dylan Thomas that their genius impels them to explore such areas, with an enormous consequent release of energy, at whatever cost to their own personal lives.

From what has been said so far, I hope it is clear that writing this monograph has represented, for me, and mapped, a series of personal discoveries; and for this reason I have thought it proper to introduce it with a retrospective outline of my own involvement in the material.

I

Thomas and Richards: Patterns of Influence

In 1945, when Richards was first invited to illustrate Thomas's poems, he was already forty-two (eleven years older than Thomas), and a mature, accomplished artist with many strong, original works behind him – for example, his *Relief Constructions*, particularly *Two Females* (1937-8), the oil-painting *The Female Contains All Qualities* (1937; fig. 43), his series on *The Sculptor and his Studio*, and his lyrical *Costers* series. These spanned the nineteen-thirties, a period of high output and achievement for him.

Richards was born in Dunvant, near Swansea, on June 6th 1903. His father, who directed the local chapel choir, instilled a love of poetry and music in him from an early age, and he later became an accomplished pianist. "After painting," Roberto Sanesi writes, "music was second nature to him",[1] and musical influences are paramount in many of his compositions, particularly his series of works relating to Debussy and Beethoven. From 1920 to 1924 Richards studied at the Swansea School of Art, and from 1924 to 1927 at the Royal College of Art in London. By the early to mid 'thirties, he had absorbed the achievements and experiments of most of the major twentieth century art movements into his work: Cubism, Dada, Surrealism and so on. Arp, Picasso, Ernst, Matisse and Kandinsky had all had profound influences on him. As Sanesi points out, his range was always eclectic. He travelled swiftly through differing modes, and he always operated cyclically and organically, often returning to explore styles and themes which he had already worked through systematically years before. "Richards seems to have been permanently in advance of his time, in that the zones and modes of expression he tackled were nearly always out of step with prevailing fashions at the moment they revealed themselves to him; and whether deliberately or otherwise, he would always drop them to go off in other directions precisely at that point when they became a *fait accompli*."[2]

For these reasons, it cannot be claimed that Thomas was in any way a 'formative' influence on Richards. By 1945, his apprenticeship was long over; a very wide range of influences had been assimilated by him; and his position as one of the leading British artists of his generation was already well established. Thomas's effect on him must be described in a different way: rather as 'transformative', that is, as an intensifying and deepening of his powers, and as an increasing in his own awareness of them at a time when he was already mature, so that he felt confident and ready to explore any theme he chose, however portentous in content or dynamic in its release of energies. There are some creative artists who appear fully fledged in their youth: Keats, Rimbaud, and Dylan Thomas himself, among whose first published poems, in 1933, at the age of nineteen, was the near perfect lyric 'The force that through the green fuse drives the flower'. As often as not, such people burn themselves out quickly. Richards was not made in that mould: his development was slow and plant-like, increasing steadily into his maturity and rooting gradually but more firmly into deeper and deeper imaginative strata.

Of his work of the 'thirties, John Russell has written as follows:

> Ceri Richards's relief constructions were among the most substantial of British contributions to the modern movement. They were both strong and taut, in formal terms. They were continuously and exuberantly resourceful in their use of the most heterogeneous materials. In many cases they showed a developed humane curiosity about other beings. They had Ceri Richards's own arrowy intelligence and free-running sense of fun. They were beautifully made, with a perfectionist craftsmanship not always found in avant-garde work.[3]

This is high praise and an apt description. But it is noticeable how the main emphasis here is on aspects of craft and technique, and how, when it comes to content, Russell confines himself to commenting on qualities that are more or less cerebral: "humane curiosity", "arrowy intelligence" and "free-running sense of fun". Little is implied either about the *power* of these works, about any element in them which sparks off a direct and unfiltered *feeling* response in the viewer, or any possible significance they might have to a person even marginally outside the cultured élite: fellow artists 'in the know' about avant-garde movements, elegant fellow-critics and well-heeled art-buyers. It is all in the mind, and one comes away from

24

this passage, as from many of the works themselves, with the sense that for all their qualities, during this period Richards was something of a painter's painter: witty, elegant, resourceful and a master of his techniques, but still rather self-contained, working out problems which were largely aesthetic and with, as yet, no more than the subliminal smouldering of his full imaginative fire. Of course, it is only meaningful to make such an assessment as this with hindsight, once the entire corpus of an artist, achieved gradually through time, has been laid out – as it were, spatially, as in a map – which is to say, after his death. Nor do I mean to belittle Richards's work of the 'thirties. In retrospect it is clear that he was far from marking time in this period: many of these works link strongly with his later and, in my view, richer post-war development; all of them built foundations for it; and some, particularly *The Female Contains All Qualities, Two Females* and the studies of costermen and women and of pearly kings and queens, have an authority, exuberance, lightness of touch and humane warmth all of their own, as Russell's comment implies; although it must also be added that these pieces possess another quality too, which is characteristic of all his best work, and is hardly hinted at in Russell's description of the relief constructions: a strong undercurrent of erotic suggestiveness, which often rises openly to the surface. But on the whole, I think it is true to say that Richards was working gradually outwards through self-imposed limitations on both form and content in the 'thirties, that it was a time of conscious stylistic experimentation for him, and that he had not yet fully 'opened up'. Even the titles of the works in *The Sculptor and his Studio* series bear this out: *The Sculptor and his Model, The Artist and his Object, The Sculptor Contemplating his Model,* and so on (see, for example, fig. 45). They suggest a somewhat closeted and indrawn preoccupation, despite their technical virtuosity, their variety of human content and abstract form, the constant erotic suggestion in the objects and models themselves, and the ease and gracefulness many of them radiate. Their inner exuberance is tightly harnessed. More important, although both their symbolism and inner direction are clearly apparent now in the light of his whole later development, they do not appear to have been fully comprehended by Richards at the time. It is as though he had to paint 'in order to find out what he had to paint', and understand it later: not an unusual phenomenon among creative artists. In Sanesi's words, "the great period of the reliefs" was "a fulfilled and happy time, if not fully understood", and he goes on to say of Richards's later productions of the 'thirties, that:

> These works already indicate the two major currents that run through all of Richards's work: his profound concern with the human presence, what one might term the 'anthropomorphic' quality of his vision; and perhaps even more important, his strong sense of the pantheistic and dionysian forces at work in all the metamorphoses of the physical and natural world, together with his awareness of the power of eroticism and of the female principle.[4]

Gradually through the war, however, Richards's work did open up. It became more fluid, eloquent and out-of-doors, and fantasy was given fuller and fuller rein. A 1944 painting entitled *Cycle of Nature* shows his transition and, as its title suggests, also his concern with "the metamorphoses of the physical and natural world", which anticipates his work relating to Thomas. The treatment is expressly symbolic. A mass of teeming, turbulent growth spreads over the canvas, all of it in some way or other suggesting the fertility of plant and animal life, as well as struggle, violence and aggressive sexuality, as if these had been held down below the surface but were now unleashed explosively, perhaps by the war. At the same time, however, the painting has lost much of the precision and focus of his earlier, more geometrical work. There is nothing contained about its images. It is full of life, but the life in it sprawls, almost in riot.

Coinciding with the end of the war, and coming shortly after his *Cycle of Nature* series, the contact with Dylan Thomas could not have come at a better time, as can be seen from his first treatment of a poem by Thomas, 'The force that through the green fuse drives the flower', which Tambimuttu commissioned from Richards for Volume 3 of his magazine *Poetry London* in 1945, sensing the appropriateness of inviting a Welsh artist to illustrate the work of a Welsh poet. The result turned out to be far more than a happy accident. Richards did three colour lithographs: two single pages using short quotations from the poem beneath swirling, symbolic designs, and a double-page centrepiece incorporating the entire text in his flowing handwriting, the whole triptych full of turbulent, eddying images of fertilisation, fruition and death (figs. 40-42). Since the theme of the poem tallied perfectly with his own preoccupations in *The Cycle of Nature*, Richards's lithographs were more than just good illustrations, intelligent readings or sensitive interpretations, though they were all of these too. These had an energy, explosiveness, *duende* all of their own, but also of Thomas's own kind. Here was the same flickering sheen of humour and gusto as Thomas's; the same underlying morbidity, wryness, introspection and longing; the same facility for tight compositional structure that could still contain a profusion of inter-connecting images; and the same central concern: celebration of life, the wheel, the eternal round, eros and mortality: love defeating death defeating love defeating death. And the same witty, daring, outrageous games that Thomas had turned and twisted through his verbal puns and syntactic dances, here Richards was also patterning with his own visual ambiguities and rhythms. Here were bulbs that were simultaneously electric life-givers, soil-embedded onions and the torso and womb of a subterranean or submarine female figure whose buttocks and thighs reached down through clay into bedrock, the whole image germinating and dividing into cotyledons which also suggested lampshades, whirlwinds, tears, seeds, grapes, figs, breasts, a skull's empty eye sockets, testicles and the ventricles of a heart. Here too was a meristematic tap root which was also an eel, fish, snake-head, phallus and human foot, and another which was both an electric wire and a tail like that of a sting ray. Here were leaved, flowering plants which became table-lamps or standard lamps, cabbalistic trees of life, alchemical alembics, and the fertile, erotic bodies of women whose sexuality and spirituality were celebrated as one glorious indivisible unity.

The forms of these central figures are so close to that of his 1937-8 relief, *Two Females,* and to the much more exuberant monochrome lithograph of 1947 with the same title (fig. 44), that the explicit celebration of female sexuality and generative power in them cannot possibly be doubted. Here, though, the treatment is far less restrained and abstract than in previous paintings, and symbolism has been taken on, lyrically, as a deliberate and explicit mode to link up different layers of meaning. Clearly, the artist here was tapping the same creative and destructive 'force' that the poet has been listening in to, and speaking about and out from; and, what is more, was now consciously *aware* that he was doing so. This awareness adds dimensions of depth to images which otherwise would have been merely spontaneous and self-expressive, or else formal and abstract. In this way, just as in a 'metaphysical' conceit in a poem by John Donne – who, incidentally, had a profound effect on Thomas – emotion and thought are yoked together. As Roberto Sanesi has written of Thomas's poem 'In the White Giant's Thigh': "Così la poesia diventa anche . . . una metafora dell'atto creativo." (*Thus poetry also becomes . . . a metaphor for the act of creation.*)[5] In these illustrations, as in all of Richards's best work, this is true for painting too; and from 1945 on, he consistently takes up the challenge implied in Thomas's line in 'If I were tickled by the rub of love': "Man be my metaphor."[6] Incidentally, the use of quotations from Thomas's poems as formal elements in Richards's design here is repeated with even greater effect in later works (e.g. in figs. 23 and 25, and in the 1965 *Dylan Thomas Suite* of lithographs[7]).

Like any good artist, Richards received his themes, gratefully, from wherever they presented themselves, and submitted himself to many different influences and disciplines throughout his life. But for the twenty-six years following the end of World War II, when he was producing his finest work, he returned again and again to Dylan Thomas's poems, re-interpreting them, commenting upon them, re-creating them, and always making them into something fresh and new. In Sanesi's words again: "From that time on his work based upon the texts of his friend became fully integrated into his own creative experience, and one of his central concerns."[8] Using titles, themes, images or motifs from Thomas's work, he produced rough sketches and finished drawings, temperas and lithographs, watercolours and gouaches, a theatre set and oil-paintings. The three colour lithographs for *Poetry London* in 1945 were followed by two oil-paintings in the same year, also based on the same poem. These were followed in 1952 by the *Afal du Brogŵyr* water-colour study and oil-painting, and in 1953 by the four sets of drawings made in the *Collected Poems*, of which *DPDT* is one. In February 1954 he designed the scenery for the *Dylan Thomas Memorial Reading* organised by the Sunday Times at the Globe Theatre, London, and between 1953 and 1955 he did more oil-paintings, black and white lithographs and drawings, with titles like *Requiem for Dylan Thomas, Homage to Dylan Thomas* and *Do not go gentle into that good night* (see figs. 23-26). A whole decade later, in 1965, there followed the *Dylan Thomas Suite* lithographs; and in many of these he returned to poems he had already treated, including 'The force that through the green fuse drives the flower' and 'Do not go gentle into that good night' (fig. 27). In 1964-5 he also executed at least a dozen oil-paintings with titles like *The Crooked Rose, Cycle of Nature, Root and Flower, Flora Breasted*, etc., all of which derive from *The Cycle of Nature* series and the *The force that through the green fuse drives the flower* of 1944-5, and integrate the cyclic, regenerative themes which Thomas himself explored. Many other works from this last great period reveal the unity of art and nature, treated lyrically as metaphors for each other, which Richards had also encountered in Thomas: *Green Image* and *Metamorphosis* (1967), *Leaves of Grass, Summer* and *The Seasons* (1968), *Harvest* and *Blossoming Tree – Male and Female* (1969), and *Origin of Species* (1971, fig. 46). As the titles show, this was a time of flowering for Richards in every sense. And among the very last works he produced, in 1971, when he was depressed and unwell and only weeks before his death, was a series of nine line-drawings commissioned for the Folio Society's edition of *Under Milk Wood*, which was published posthumously in 1972. Although these have a studied quality, and perhaps lack the spontaneity or exuberance of his best paintings or drawings, they are delicate, warmly human, witty and affectionate, and a harmonious close to a prolific career.

This long list of works relating wholly or partially to Thomas is not exhaustive, since it does not include a number of paintings and innumerable sketches, for Richards was always sketching on any bit of paper that came to hand, including the backs of old envelopes. But it is convincing evidence of Thomas's importance to Richards, even without our exploring in detail the recurrence of similar visual themes and motifs which are not even indirectly related to the works of the poet. For present purposes, Sanesi's remarks are a fitting commentary: that this represents ". . . an enormous output in terms of the whole of his artistic corpus, and one that was extraordinarily fertile in a number of quite different ways".[9] I would go even further: In my view, Thomas's work is not merely "one of Richards's central concerns", but takes us right into the core of Richards's own artistic genius. And I would suggest that it did so in four separate but related ways. Firstly (although this was equally true of other influences), Thomas's work provided him with 'objective correlatives', validating and extending his own 'subjective' images. Secondly, the combination of vitality, experimentation and formal constraints in the poems themselves, with their total mastery over rhythm, gave him fuller scope to express his own exuberance within the constraints of his own meticulously developed craftsmanship, and so helped bring the elegant skill of his work in the 'thirties and the explosiveness of his work in the war years together into a new synthesis from which he never looked back. Thirdly, in Thomas, Richards found images and themes which echoed the experiences of his own boyhood in South Wales – the hills and sea, the gulls and herons, the clouds and suns, the seasons passing in an intimately recognisable way – and by re-activating his own long-term memories, all of this enabled him "to travel back / And tread again that ancient track" into those childhood experiences which the Welsh seventeenth century poet Henry Vaughan speaks of,[10] to discover "bright shootes of everlastingnesse" among them, and to tap these more and more fully in his work. And fourthly, and perhaps most important, the metaphysical and symbolist elements in Thomas's poetry, combining with these familiar and natural images, helped him towards a fuller understanding both of the inner connectedness among his personal themes, and also of their potential to communicate complex meanings transpersonally; that is to say, of their potential as *symbols*. It is as a symbolist painter that Richards's mature work is most powerful and demands to be read, and Thomas's influence was paramount in bringing this development about.

Thomas's work, therefore, operated on Richards not by teaching him anything new, but rather, it 'reminded' him of what he knew already. It validated and helped him articulate more clearly what he already had in him, objectifying what was latent or only partially conscious, and extending what was still subjective into the communal realm of symbol: into a zone which could belong (and in fact, always does belong) to everybody. In doing this, it released passions and energies in him which he could explore without either fear or the need to repress them, and this led him to confrontation with archetypal material which Carl Gustav Jung was quick to recognise, and to which he was able to give form in increasingly clear, fluent images of eros, fertility and death. Thus the overall result of his contact with Thomas's work in 1945 was that, whatever the stated context or subject matter of all his works which followed, and however varied they were in reference or treatment, from that time on one single, coherent, deep theme coursed through every one of them; and this was precisely Thomas's own central obsession: celebration of the fecundity, transformative power and creativity of art itself both as a manifestation and metaphor of the cyclic pattern of nature, embodied above all in sexuality. Thomas's poems, then, *transformed* Richards's art and, in doing so, they also brought him directly into contact with the continuous process of transformation within himself which is the key to all artistic creation: to that 'turning point', into a state of

30

'unforgetting', described by Erich Neumann as follows:

> *. . . What happens here is what happens at the beginning of time: the creation of the world . . .* And . . . in this primordial act of having become creative, of world creation, such a 'turning point' is achieved, in which creator and creature, as well as the acts of being begotten and born and becoming creative, merge with one another. *The creative process is generation and birth as well as transformation and rebirth. As the Chinese said: "Transformation is the creation of creating."* The rapture of him who pours forth like a spring is reflected in the serenity of the creation. The perpetual self-renewal and dependence on grace of him who pours forth eternally are a human parallel to the eternal rebirth of all that is created. The rapture of the flowing deathlessness of creativity is just as much at work in man as in nature; indeed, it is only in his creative flowing that man becomes a part of nature, is joined again to the 'one reality' of existence, in which no enduring thing can endure, because all is transformation. (Italics mine, R.B.)[11]

II

Coincidences and Correspondences

---

1 'SEA SON OF THE WAVE'

Curious 'coincidences' connect the dates of Richards's composition of the
DPDT series with those of both Thomas's death and his own, which, in the
context of the striking images of death which recur in a number of the
drawings, deserve commenting on. On the 'credits page', facing the poet's
dedication of the book to his wife, Richards has written in his characteristically flowing script, 'Drawings made on November 7-8-'53', and below
that, his signature. The drawings were made in the studio at his home in
Edith Grove, Chelsea. Under the photograph of Augustus John's portrait of
Dylan Thomas, which is the frontispiece to the *Collected Poems*, Richards
later wrote 'Died November 9 1953'. Here the year is not abbreviated but
given in full, and the smaller, tighter script suggests a more reflecting,
pensive state of mind than the broad penstrokes of the earlier script, which
have the same exuberance as many of the drawings.

These observations are full of curiosity not only because the drawings
were made in London just one day before Dylan Thomas died, aged 39, in
New York, without any possibility of Richards having any conscious
foreknowledge of the poet's impending death (even if it is possible that he
knew that Thomas was ill), but because the artist's recording of the precise
dates in this manner, and as an integral part of his text, suggests that
afterwards he sensed connections between that event and his composition
which were meaningful to him. Just as curious is the fact that Richards
himself died on 9th November, of a sudden heart attack, eighteen years to
the day after Thomas, in 1971, and that in his jacket-pocket at the time was
a copy of Thomas's poems. Frances Richards, who is one of the least
superstitious people I know, made a special point of emphasising these
patterns of dates to me when she first showed me the book in November

1976, as if she too sensed at least the possibility of significant relationships among them. And even the most rigorously sceptical and empirically minded of readers is likely, I would suggest, to register in the timing of these drawings' composition an unusual human poignancy which gives them the special status of a testament.

It is also interesting that Thomas and Richards hardly knew each other personally. Sanesi speaks of Richards's "work based on the texts of his friend",[1] but although Richards was born in Dunvant, near Swansea, on June 6th 1903, and Thomas was born in Swansea itself, only a few miles away, on October 27th 1914, and although they both shared close friends in the poet Vernon Watkins and the painter Alfred Janes, they only actually met on one occasion, not long before Thomas's death. To establish these facts I taped an interview with Frances Richards in June 1977, and this is her account:

> Ceri never really knew Dylan. He only met him once, and that was the day before Dylan went to America. Dylan was very quiet and didn't want to go. Ceri was taken down by Fred Janes, to meet Dylan and spend the day with him in Laugharne. The idea was that on Dylan's return from America, he would do a reading of his poems in the Glynn Vivian Art Gallery in Swansea, with Ceri's paintings in the background. Ceri had done a lot of work by then on Dylan's poems, and the paintings to be used were all to be those based on Dylan's poems. That was in 1953. But Dylan died in America. He never came back.

Several points of interest emerge from this statement. Firstly, it suggests that *DPDT*, and possibly also its other variants, might well have been intended by Richards as sketches for more elaborate works, in preparation for the Glynn Vivian Gallery reading and exhibition, which never materialised because of Thomas's death in America. Secondly, the fact that Richards visited Laugharne only once, and met Thomas only once, shows how quick and keen were his powers of observation and memory: the various sketches in *DPDT* of Thomas himself,[2] and of the boathouse in Laugharne on the title-page, all suggest a longer familiarity. These are points we shall return to in more detail when discussing the variants of *DPDT* in Chapter IV. More important here, however, is the fact that Richards's affinity with Thomas's work was not based on any intimate knowledge of Thomas the man: for this reason, the depth and articulateness of his response to the poems seems all the more extraordinary.

Other considerations, however, must also be explored. The struggle between *eros* and *thanatos* is as much a major theme in Thomas's poems as it is in Shakespeare's *Sonnets* or Keats's *Odes*. Poets often prefigure their own deaths in their poems, and sometimes do so with an accuracy that, in retrospect, seems uncanny. This is particularly so when both the lives and the works are tragic, and it accounts in part for the fascination the lives of such men and women exert over us. Keats himself is an example of this, as are Shelley, Rimbaud, Tsvetayeva, Mandelstam and Pavese, to list just a few. The major obsessions and dominant themes in their writings seem inextricably bound up with the patterns of destinies in their lives and, taken together, these assume the features of a struggle which appears heroic in its proportions. 'Tragedy' here is not too strong a word, as Neumann elaborates:

> . . .The next stage in the relation of art to its epoch is the stage of compensation for the cultural canon . . . Great art of this type almost necessarily implies tragedy. Compensation for the cultural canon means opposition to it – that is, opposition to the epoch's consciousness and sense of values. The creative artist, whose mission it is to compensate for consciousness and the cultural canon, is usually an isolated individual, a hero who must destroy the old in order to make possible the dawn of the new.
> . . .This perhaps is why the careers of the great artists of our time are all, in greater or lesser degree, calvaries. The task of integration facing the great artist today can no longer be performed in a single work, but more than ever before requires a unity of life and work.[3]

It is interesting to note in passing here that "destroying the old in order to make possible the dawn of the new" implicitly allocates to the great artist the role of cultural *revolutionary,* even if this is not recognised by the artist's contemporaries. Aside from this, as any biography of Thomas will show, he took enormous pleasure in flouting the cultural canon, though always operating within the context of tradition, both in the diction of his poems and in eccentricities of personal behaviour, childish though some of the latter may have seemed to the conventionally minded. It is also well known that Thomas's death was precipitated, and probably directly caused, by alcoholism. I would suggest that the most apt metaphor for this condition might well be *drowning:* the alcoholic 'drowns his sorrows' in drink, 'drowns in despair' and so on, and, in a very real sense, might be said to be drowning himself in his own life. Even a superficial reading of Thomas's poems shows that the sea was an enormously strong shaping presence in his life and work. Imagery of water abounds, as do images of sailing, fishing, swimming, diving and drowning, and these are particularly predominant in the last poems. In 'Elegy', for example, we find: "I saw / Through his unseeing eyes to the roots of the sea."[4] 'Poem on his birthday' ends with the line: "As I sail out to die",[5] and 'Fern Hill' too ends with: "Time held me green and dying / Though I sang in my chains like the sea."[6] 'Lament' contains the lines: "Whenever I dove in a breast high shoal, / . . . Black night, I left my quivering prints."[7] Many more examples could be given, but one of the most interesting of all the poems containing sea-imagery is the difficult 'Ballad of the Long-legged Bait', whose whole theme is concerned with drowning in "the graveyard of the water":

> Down, down, down, under the ground,
> Under the floating villages,
> Turns the moon-chained and water-wound
> Metropolis of fishes . . .[8]

Richards too explored sea-images, shared from his own Welsh boyhood, in at least ten drawings in *DPDT*,[9] which suggests an appropriate reading of the poems at a 'deep' symbolic level; and he also took up the theme of sea-engulfment again later, in his treatment of the Breton legend of the drowned island *Ys*, in his *La Cathédrale Engloutie* series.[10] The image of the cathedral buried under the waves, whose spire sometimes rises above them and whose bells can be heard chiming on a clear day, also recurs in several of Thomas's poems, including the 'Ballad of the Long-legged Bait':

> She longs among horses and angels,
> The rainbow-fish bend in her joys,
> Floated the lost cathedral
> Chimes of the rocked buoys . . .

and

> Over the wakeward-flashing spray
> Over the gardens of the floor
> Clash out the mounting dolphin's day
> My mast is a bell-spire . . .[11]

Similarly, and noting the apt pun on the word 'masses', in 'Ceremony After a Fire Raid' we find that: "Into the organpipes and steeples / Of the luminous cathedrals . . ."

> . . .The masses of the sea under
> The masses of the infant-bearing sea
> Erupt, fountain, and enter to utter forever
> Glory glory glory
> The sundering ultimate kingdom of genesis' thunder.[12]

In this context, there is also a curious connection between Thomas's Christian name and another 'Dylan' in Welsh mythology, the firstborn son of a lady called Arianrod in the story entitled 'Math Son of Mathonwy' in *The Mabinogion*, of whom it is told that:

> The boy was baptised, and the moment he was baptised he made for the sea. And there and then, as soon as he came to the sea he received the sea's nature, and swam as well as the best fish in the sea. And for that reason he was called Dylan Eil Ton.[13]

The meaning of the Welsh name 'Dylan Eil Ton' is 'Sea Son of the Wave'. And, even more interestingly, the boy dies by drowning. It hardly seems likely that Dylan Thomas was ignorant of either the etymology of his own name or its sources in this myth, but at any rate, both the patterns of imagery in his poems and the facts leading to his own death reveal an almost uncanny correspondence to it. Equally interestingly, other parts of this story reveal correspondences with Richards's work based on Thomas, through the motif of the flower-maiden who was turned into an owl. We shall return to this, and to the symbolism of sea-related images, in Chapters IV and V.

As for the struggle between *eros* and *thanatos*, it is also well known that Thomas viewed the act of poetic composition itself, in the same traditional way as the Shakespeare of the *Sonnets* and Keats, as one fully aligned with the forces of light, love and life against those of darkness, destruction and death. This tenet of his poetic faith can be traced in the abundant imagery of sun and light in his poems. In 'How soon the servant sun', for example, he describes himself in the first person as: "All nerves to serve the sun / The rite of light".[14] There is also a tendency in many poems to move towards a last line containing an apocalyptic image of light, often pictured as the sun or flames: e.g. "And a hundred storks perch on the sun's right hand." in 'Among those Killed in the Dawn Raid Was a Man Aged a Hundred';[15] "And you shall wake, from country sleep, this dawn and each first dawn, / Your faith as deathless as the outcry of the ruled sun" in 'In Country Sleep';[16] "And the daughters of darkness flame like Fawkes fires still" in 'In

36

the white giant's thigh';[17] "And the dark thrown / From his loin / to bright / Light" and "Now I am lost in the blinding / One. The sun roars at the poem's end" in 'Vision and Prayer'[18]; and in the last stanza of 'I dreamed my genesis' (see front cover, and figs. 37 and 38). A line in 'Poem on his birthday' expresses this movement perfectly: "Dark is a way and light is a place."[19] In 'Find meat on bones', the tension between these forces is resolved, albeit momentarily, in the lines: "Light and dark are no enemies / But one companion."[20] But the usual expression of the theme is in terms of conflict, as in the famous refrains of his villanelle written on the death of his father: "Do not go gentle into that good night. / Rage, rage against the dying of the light."[21] Sun-and sea-images often occur together in the poems, and the symbolic resonances of this association, which is an integral one, will be explored in Chapter V. In general, though, where the struggle for light against darkness ends in failure, the tendency is for the poem to end in an image of drowning; where it is successful, the sun indeed "roars at the poem's end".

From all these images, it is clear that through all his various 'masks' – of witty buffoon, bombastic word-spinner, wild boozer and eccentric bohemian – Thomas regarded both the act of writing poetry and his own social role as a poet with the utmost seriousness, as a spiritual discipline whose goal was enlightenment and revelation both for himself and for his readers; and in this respect he is an heir to the visionary tradition of Blake, Yeats and Rimbaud – a tradition which in turn derives in very large measure from gnosticism and alchemy. The 'Note' written in November 1952 which prefaces his *Collected Poems* hints at this:

> I read somewhere of a shepherd who, when asked why he made, from within fairy rings, ritual observances to the moon to protect his flocks, replied: 'I'd be a damn' fool if I didn't!' These poems, with all their crudities, doubts and confusions, are written for the love of Man and in praise of God, and I'd be a damn' fool if they weren't.[22]

The casual, almost flippant tone here (perhaps a necessary 'mask' to avoid any connotations of pompous priestliness) should not blind us to the fact that Thomas's analogy is not only fancifully 'magical' but also *religious:* the poet is seen as the shepherd of men who protects his flock by his ritual incantations. But the idea is elaborated most clearly in his reply to the questionnaire sent out by the editors of *New Verse* to its contributors in October 1934, which Thomas completed when he was just over twenty years old, a few days before a trip to London on November 11th that year. To the bland question, "Do you intend your poetry to be useful to yourself or others?" Thomas replied in a manner as precise and assured as it was humble and inspired:

> To both. Poetry is the rhythmic, inevitably narrative, movement from an overclothed blindness to a naked vision that depends in its intensity on the strength of the labour put into the creation of the poetry. *My poetry is, or should be, useful to me for one reason: it is the record of my individual struggle from darkness towards some measure of light,* and what of the individual struggle is still to come benefits by the sight and knowledge of the faults and fewer merits in that concrete record. *My poetry is, or should be, useful to others for its individual recording of that same struggle with which they are necessarily acquainted.* (Italics mine, R.B.)[23]

The lyrics in which this struggle is most nakedly explicit are probably 'The force that through the green fuse drives the flower', 'I dreamed my genesis', 'And death shall have no dominion', 'Do not go gentle into that good night', and 'In My Craft or Sullen Art'. These all celebrate the individual's repeated attempts to embody true creativity within himself or herself, and the constant pull of opposing forces that are in conflict with this upward thrust, both within and without. They are among Thomas's finest and best known poems, and Richards has responded to each of them with drawings in *DPDT*, some of which are the most haunting in the whole series. For two out of the five poems listed here, as well as for one other, 'The bread I break', a pattern of imagery emerges in the visual designs which extracts the darkest and most frightening elements from the verses and offers a commentary on them which appears particularly apt in the context of Thomas's own impending death. As in the poems themselves, images of death and decay are starkly contrasted and ambivalently merged with totally opposing images of fertility and growth. In these three drawings the dominant motif is the death's head.

2   SKULLS AND FLOWERS

In the design that frames 'This bread I break' (fig. 17), a skull with black eye-sockets, and the lower jaw missing, perches in the bottom right hand corner on a table on top of two thick tomes, crowned by a bunch of grapes.

Above it, or growing out of it, is a vine, with leaves and more bunches of grapes towering profusely upwards, while lines suggesting the forms of ears of corn, and possibly also quills (echoing the front-cover design for *DPDT*, fig. 1), balance the left hand side of the poem. On the table is also a long stemmed wineglass. Keats's sonnet 'When I have fears that I may cease to be'[24] is called strongly to mind by this drawing, with its "high piled books, in charactery" that "hold like rich garners the full ripened grain" harvested from the poet's "teeming brain". Diagonal and curved lines in the piece suggest both upward and downward movements, growth and decay, and there is a fine balance between them. However, the poem itself is not a particularly pessimistic one and contains no skulls or direct references to death: it is rather a celebration of the sacramental and transcendental power of poetry as an agent of the spirit that redeems and renews the life of the body. It uses the archaic imagery of sacrifice underlying Christian mass and communion to explore the Romantic notion that the poet, like Christ, Attis, Tammuz or Adonis, gives out spiritual nourishment and strength by the outpouring of his own life-spirit, into his verses: "My wine you drink, my bread you snap." Hints of dark elements are present, in the breaking of the poet's body and the letting of his blood, but the overall tone is confident and positive, although the theme is conventional and I do not think the poem is one of Thomas's best. The visual emphasis in Richards's drawing, though, is much more eerie. In the bold, intense lines of the skull itself and in the sharp criss-cross shading around it, one's attention is drawn insistently to the fact of mortality and is made to dwell there. The drawing celebrates death himself (or herself?) as the king (or queen?) of grapes and wine – an appropriate testament indeed for a poet who drank himself to death.

The drawing for 'And death shall have no dominion' (fig. 19; and compare figs. 18 and 20) is if anything even more powerful: here too a skull occupies the bottom right-hand corner of the design. It is implanted in weeds and rubble, with long, leafy stems sprouting directly out of the two eye-sockets, from which grow black, lily or iris-like flowers and, by contrast, one small, white sun-shaped, daisy-like flower, struggling to assert its head below the others. The 'lines of force' which Richards uses in many of these drawings to indicate paths of energy are deployed here to suggest both a single, inevitable, rhythmic and cyclic process working through all natural phenomena, and also enormous upheaval and conflict of wills within this overall pattern. The whirling, turbulent auras moving upwards around the heads of the flowers contrast with other equally strong diagonal lines: those bordering the poem on the left-hand side might also suggest an upward, expansive movement, though they could equally well represent falling rain; but those at the top of the design press downwards from above the clouds and are emphasised by the line of descent of a plummeting white bird. All these motifs aptly echo lines in the poem, particularly in the last stanza:

> No more may gulls cry at their ears
> Or waves break loud on the seashores;
> Where blew a flower may a flower no more
> Lift its head to the blows of the rain;
> Though they be mad and dead as nails,
> Heads of the characters hammer through daisies;
> Break in the sun till the sun breaks down,
> And death shall have no dominion.

Looked at in one way, the treatment of the life-death struggle is more positive here than for 'This bread I break': plants grow openly out of the skull's eye-sockets and life is determinedly rooted in death – just as in the poem, "heads of the characters hammer through daisies". (Another Keatsian echo?) But while affirmative elements are present, five out of the six flowers are black, and once again the dominant image is the skull. It is an uneasy and ambivalent picture and hardly an unequivocal celebration of the resurrection of the dead, which is what, perhaps in a rather facile way, I had taken to be the central meaning of the poem until I saw Richards's drawing. "A little flower is the labour of ages," said Blake, but one cannot help wondering how many skulls need to be planted in the soil to make the flowers grow. And if it were not for the saving grace of that single, small daisy head, one might well be forgiven for wondering if these were not *fleurs du mal* pushing up out of the skull – poisoned, ill-omened and festering – and whether the prime-mover directing their growth towards the sky were not the Lord (or Lady?) of Darkness rather than the Lord (or Lady?) of Light. By my reading, the drawing offsets the poem by asserting, in similarly riddling and equivocal terms, that Death indeed *does* have dominion, even in the midst of life; and it does so by confronting unflinchingly the ugliness, pain and terror underlying the most ephemeral and fragile of beauty. As Rilke wrote in the *Duino Elegies*:

40

For Beauty's nothing
but beginning of terror we're still just able to bear,
and why we adore it so is because it serenely
disdains to destroy us. [25]

Whether my interpretation is correct or not, however, just as for 'This bread I break', Richards's design here is an entirely suitable, if startling commentary on the poem, germinating seeds deep in its core and uncovering chthonic forces among its roots in both his own and the poet's imagination. This design, incidentally, is also worth comparing with Richards's treatment of the same poem in his 1965 series of lithographs, [26] and with his 1953-5 works relating to Thomas (figs. 23-25). [27] Here, skulls and flowers also appear, along with herons, but the treatment is far more harmonious and peaceful, even elegiac. The heron probably derives initially from the 'Author's Prologue', 'Poem on his birthday' and 'Over Sir John's Hill' and already figures in Richards's drawing for the last of these poems in *DPDT* (fig. 21), as it does even more prominently in several drawings in the Swansea variant of the *Collected Poems*, also executed in November 1953 (figs. 20 and 22). Richards developed many of his major themes in cycles, and for this precise reason his drawings do not isolate the poems but connect them: images are often transposed from one poem to another, so that they can be 'read' as a unified sequence with their own inner coherence while also providing a systematic interpretative commentary on the poems themselves.

The third drawing in the book with a skull image frames the poem 'The force that through the green fuse drives the flower' (fig. 11), and this is particularly interesting when contrasted with his 1945 treatments (figs. 40-42, already discussed) and the 1965 lithographs based on the poem.[28] Similar or related motifs are used on each occasion, but the treatments are very different, and the most startling of them all is the line-drawing in *DPDT*, even though the others are richer and more finely worked. Here, the dominant image, occupying the whole space on the right hand side of the poem, is a black winding sheet (the "shroud sail" in the third stanza of the poem), which is both slung from the branches of a tree, like an eerie piece of witch's washing hung out to dry; and also simultaneously seems to support it, so that the sheet is identified with both the bark of the tree and the mast of a death-ship. If there is any doubt as to the meanings of this strange and complex image, or as to Richards's conscious intentions in

41

shaping it, this can be dispelled by reference to another design for the same poem in the Swansea version (fig. 9). In this draft, which is no more than a line-sketch, the text of the poem is framed inside a tattered sheet slung between a flowering, leafy stem on the left and a hand belonging to a partly outlined naked female form on the right. In the Swansea text an almost identical design is also used for the previous-but-one poem in the *Collected Poems*, 'Before I knocked' (fig. 8), which is unillustrated in *DPDT*. It is impossible to state with any certainty the order of composition of these two versions, but basing our argument on the differing degrees of complexity of these drawings, we can conjecture that the Swansea version is likely to have been the earlier of the two and that Richards approached and developed his subject more or less as follows. At first, he tried out a relatively simple design, deriving it from the three images which had sprung at him from the poem, "the green fuse" with its "flower" in the first line, and the "hand" in stanza three, connecting them by means of the "shroud sail" two lines later, and also introducing an image of his own, the naked female form. Although this is moderately pleasing visually, the design does not work especially well either formally in its own right, or thematically in relationship to the poem. The hand and the female form in particular seem superfluous, even frivolously so, despite a deep symbolic connection between femininity and this 'tree of life and death' which goes back to Lilith and Eve in the Garden. But these images are strung together in a somewhat arbitrary fashion, so that the drawing has none of the resonance of the poem itself, whose images chime together in an insistent rhythm akin to that of a blood pulse. Either earlier or later, Richards also tried out the same design for the poem 'Before I knocked', where it did not work particularly appropriately either. But by gradually exploring these simple images, he transmuted them into the much richer and more polished drawing in the *DPDT* version, cutting out what was inappropriate (the feminine form and the hand) and expanding the image that was by now central to him, the tree that is also a mast, draped in its sombre covering of bark, shroud and drooping sail in one. If it is correct to date composition of the Swansea version before that of *DPDT* – and I think it is, as I shall elaborate later from further evidence in Chapter IV – we have here a good example of Richards's working method, and can see how close this was to Thomas's own, in the gradual movement from spontaneous and direct responses to received images, through a slow, brooding process, to a single, complex, organic image which has been

42

carefully developed and worked. In this case, Richards's brooding has intensified the symbol's power, and taken him from a charming and playfully decorative illustration to a design whose punning resonances and rhythms match those in the poem itself.

These speculations aside, however, it is also clear that here the tree is loaded with many possible meanings. Roots snake from its base leftwards across the page and flowers and leaves grow out of it, right over the text of the poem, to tumble down profusely on the other side of the page. Once again, the drawing focuses on the unitary, cyclic nature of birth, growth, decay and death and, like the poem itself, emphasises struggle and conflict within this overall process, although here the blossoms and leaves waft lightly and jauntily across the sky as if they had not a care in the world. These airborne creatures, like clouds and flying birds, recur in many other drawings and have a rich and complex symbolism of their own that is mainly positive in its associations, at least superficially, though in the language of symbolism no meaning is ever as simple as it first seems. But the tree itself here is far from being a "green fuse", and is very different from the flowing, erotic female form either of the Swansea draft or of the 'plants' in the 1945 and 1965 lithograph treatments of the poem. It has become if anything even more black, threatening and death-like than the flowers in the drawing for 'And death shall have no dominion'. And in its centre, as if either painted on it as on a pirate's sail or engraved deep into its bark, is the shape of a skull, with a nightmarish leering expression reminiscent of the horrifying apparitions seen by lost children in the haunted forests of fairy tales. Taken together with the other two skull images in 'This bread I break' and 'And death shall have no dominion', this is much more than an apt interpretation of one particular poem. It can equally well be read as a commentary on an extremely disturbed state of being, as an expression of spiritual and physical torment, while several thousand miles away, Thomas himself was within hours of "sailing out to die". It presents a picture of a death struggle, in the most naked and dramatic terms.

In pursuing these interpretations, I want to make it emphatically clear that I am not suggesting that Richards was arbitrarily imposing a pessimistic or morbid reading, or focusing on negative aspects to the exclusion of positive ones, but rather that his renderings of these poems on this occasion were all the more apt in that the presence of death and darkness in them is insistent and haunting, balanced though it is by the upward energy and thrust of opposing and complementary forces. When the skull motif reappears in Richards's later works based on Thomas's poems, it too has undergone a subtle transformation which, as we shall see in the next chapter, has further symbolic correspondences to Celtic myth which are almost astonishingly apt, through the motif of the Graal vessel. In the context of Thomas's imminent death, however, I am suggesting that in *DPDT*, Richards extracted from his poems their deepest inner meaning.[29]

One final point must be made here. The predominant conscious ethic in our society is to repress 'the facts of death', to ignore them whenever possible, just as it is to repress female sexuality. That there is a strong connection between images of death and femininity is obvious from the innumerable portrayals in our art and literature of death as a devouring mistress: Keats's 'La Belle Dame Sans Merci', Robert Graves's *The White Goddess* and Cocteau's eerie personification of her in his film *Orphée* are just a few well-known examples. This motif abounds in Celtic literature, and Richards also explored it fully, both in the *DPDT* series and in the Celtic symbol of the Owl-Maiden, which we shall discuss in Chapter V. He looks at 'the fact of death' head on, celebrating it both as fact and as *rite de passage*, to borrow Arnold van Gennep's term.[30] From both cultural and psychological points of view, the profound importance of an artist's confronting these 'facts of death' is well stated by Neumann:

> Anyone whose ears do not burn, whose eyes do not cloud over, at the thought of the concentration camps, the crematoriums, the atomic explosions which make up our reality – at the dissonances of our music, the broken, tattered forms of our painting, the lament of Dr. Faustus – is free to crawl into the shelter of the safe old methods and rot. *The rest of us must taste again the fruit of the tree of knowledge, which will redeem us from the paradise in which it is believed that man and the world are wholly good. It is true that we run the risk of choking on it. But there is no other way. We must acknowledge the evil, the blackness, the disintegration which cry to us so desperately from the art of our time, and whose presence it so desperately affirms. Paradoxical as it may sound when formulated in theological terms, it seems today that we must redeem a bit of Satan.* (Italics mine, R.B.)[31]

The fruit of this 'tree of knowledge' is engrained in its very trunk in Richards's drawing for 'The force that through the green fuse drives the flower'. As for Satan and the apple, behind these stands the even more shadowy figure of Lilith, to whom we shall also return when we explore the *Black Apple of Gower*.

III

Form and Content in the Drawings

I   STYLE AND MOTIFS

In a short memoir about her husband, published in 1973, Frances Richards had this to say:

> Ceri was always drawing. He rarely went about without a sketchbook. He would bring one downstairs with him when he had his breakfast and he often took one to bed with him at night and picked it up again to look at when he awoke. It became a habit... If he had an idea or a theme, his imagination and creative ability, together with his remarkable facility for expression would work instantly on it and the result was usually fascinating, brilliant and original... His sense of observation always impressed me. Also the rapidity with which he could summon up an image. He only had to observe and feel a thing once to be able to draw it from every aspect. His knowledge of form was sure and complex... He drew the figure from life throughout his working career. This went on at the same time as his inventive and imaginative work, so that his forms never became repetitive or dull. [1]

Many other fellow-artists and critics have also testified to Richards's quick, keen powers of observation and his remarkable ability to draw, for example Henry Moore:

> What I always admired about Ceri Richards, right from his Royal College of Art student days, was the way he could draw. More than any other British painter of his time he understood three-dimensional form and knew how to express it on a flat surface. His drawing is so assured, so full of energy and virility, that it gives his work a quality that goes way beyond charm. In fact 'charm' isn't the word for it at all: Ceri's work has authority because of his drawing... I think it is this ability to draw which gives to his painting the same boldness and assurance, which both Picasso and Matisse show in their painting, because they are both superb draughtsmen. [2]

45

DPDT provides ample evidence of Richards's extraordinary skill as a draughtsman and as an observer of forms in the world, quite apart from the power of his images to evoke responses on a symbolic level. Both these qualities are associated with other, personal ones, which Moore goes on to describe in the same piece:

> With other people there are little things that one has to excuse, or to take for granted. But with Ceri there was none of that – I never knew him to say a nasty or spiteful thing about another artist – he never showed envy or jealousy, and he was a marvellous enthusiast and appreciator. I never knew anyone who had so few faults, so few blemishes, so little that anyone could dislike. Now that he's gone, I think all of us want to say just that.[2]

This is far more than the generous and affectionate praise of a friend and fellow-artist. The very directness and simplicity of Moore's words give us an invaluable guide to what to look for in Richards's work precisely when we are exploring the most technical and 'abstract' qualities of form, draughtsmanship, and so on. As Frances Richards's comments also indicate, the technical capacity to execute drawings swiftly and accurately, and what she calls his "inventive and imaginative work", are inseparable functions of each other, and that is why Richards's art is so spontaneous and original. Hegel put this point perfectly: "Content is nothing but the conversion of form into content, and form is nothing but the conversion of content into form."[3] The kind of attentiveness that good draughtsmanship necessarily involves is in itself a spiritual quality. The purity and directness of image in the designs in *DPDT* are products of years of practice constantly maintained. Their immediacy is not that of a naif accidentally stumbling upon inspiration but the result of hard work by a dedicated master-craftsman. For these reasons, the fact that the *DPDT* series was completed in the space of twenty-four hours needs examining carefully. Their spontaneity is no less real for these considerations, but should perhaps be linked to that of the Zen master-archer who, after a lifetime of practice, can let loose his arrow from his bow as gently as "a leaf falls from a tree" and, even when blindfold or in darkness, always find the centre of the target.[4]

Several different 'styles' are present in the *DPDT* series – or rather, stages in Richards's approaches to his subjects – from the roughest of preliminary sketches to fully elaborated designs. Somewhere between these two extremes are also a large number of unadorned, unshaded line-drawings which seem perfect in themselves and would only have been fussed or spoilt by the addition of more detail or background. Clearly these were rapidly drawn and they evoke an equally immediate response from the viewer, precisely because so little is stated and so much implied. These often present the human form, and when there is a single figure it is usually female,[5] with a strong erotic suggestiveness reminiscent of Matisse. Where there are two figures, the second is usually a male lover, and in these drawings the theme sometimes repeats that of the *Rape of the Sabines* paintings of the late 'forties.[6] Richards was also fascinated by hands, which are an important compositional element in at least a dozen of these drawings (figs. 4-7, and see also 37 and 38), and they sometimes appear with no other figurative motifs.[7] These hands express a great range of emotions, from love and affection to tension or rage, from resignation, fear and despair to abandonment in sleep or contemplation in prayer (for example, figs. 12, 13, 30 and 31).

However, these simple line-drawings are sometimes non-figurative, or, if there is a figurative element in them, they contain patterns of recurrent abstract forms. One of these is the hourglass, which is picked up, obviously, in the unfinished but interesting labyrinth-sketch for one of the hourglass-shaped poems in 'Vision and Prayer',[8] and also recurs as a minor motif in the poet's tie on the front cover (fig. 1), in the wineglass beneath 'This bread I break' (fig. 17), and in the strange shadow lurking in the sea beneath the 'black apple' (see the front cover of this book). This jagged, angular form is also echoed in repeated images of gulls, particularly beneath 'Especially when the October wind' and on the back cover design (figs. 1 and 2, and see also figs. 18, 20 and 28), contrasting with the curvilinear shapes of clouds. A large number of drawings also contain 'lines of force'. These have a function both formal and meaningful. They denote the paths and concentrations of energy currents, and they move and collect in every direction and pattern imaginable: from the whirling centripetal coil and centrifugal flames for 'Deaths and Entrances' (fig. 34) to the vertical, falling lines for the 'Author's Prologue' (fig. 7); from the dense criss-cross shading around the skull under 'This bread I break' (fig. 17) or around and above the figure of the sleepy poet (fig. 3) to the diagonal wind current for 'Especially when the October wind' (fig. 2). It is almost as if Richards could actually see at a glance not only the exact features of a physical object or event in the outside world, but also the invisible forces moving around and within it which Wilhelm Reich called 'bio-energy' and 'cosmic energy', or as though he were also a master of Blake's visionary technique: "I question not my Corporeal or Vegetative Eye any more than I would Question a Window concerning a Sight. I look thro' it & not with it."[9]

2   SUN, BLOSSOM, RAIN, CLOUDS

Perhaps the most important recurrent abstract form is the circle. This is present in the suns (figs. 32-35), in the various heads and skulls, is a minor motif in the armour-plating worn by the tired warrior for 'O make me a mask' (fig. 15), and is elaborated most forcefully as the mandala of the 'black apple' (front cover, and see also figs. 36-39). The circle always epitomises unity, identity, completion or perfection,[10] and also has a functional importance both compositional and thematic. Circles are also the abstract motifs underlying the frequent clouds and blossoms, and the common formal attribute which links them symbolically to suns. This is perhaps seen most clearly in the comical, child-like design for 'Here in this Spring' (fig. 28), where clouds and blossoms are almost entirely identified. The presence of blossoms as positive, life-bearing symbols in the design for 'The force that through the green fuse drives the flower' (fig. 11) has already been noted, but they are also to be identified *with the poet's own words*, both by implication in this drawing, where they sprout and pour profusely from his dark 'tree of life and death', but also on the front cover-design (fig. 1), where the flowers growing directly out of the poet's quill seem to turn into the clouds and seagulls which float above the embracing lovers, with "their arms/Round the griefs of the ages"[11] on the back cover, and to whom his words are addressed in the key poem 'In my Craft or Sullen Art' (fig. 3). The symbolic identification between flowers and words is borne out even more strongly by the first two designs for the 'Author's Prologue' (figs. 6 and 7, and see also fig. 4): in the first, blossoms pour downwards like manna from the page the poet is writing on, accompanied by lines of force which suggest rain, and in the second, the poet's hand sprays lines of energy (rain again?) down through the text of the poem itself. Circular flowers and the straight lines of the rain offset each other as complementary *yin* and *yang* principles. These blossoms are reminiscent of the windblown autumnal leaves in Shelley's 'Ode to the West Wind': ghosts that "quicken a new birth", which are identified with the poet's "dead thoughts" which he wishes the breath of inspiration to "Scatter, as from an unextinguished hearth" in the form of "ashes and sparks, *my words* among mankind".[12] (Italics mine, R.B.) All these images – words, wind-blown blossoms and seeds, leaves, rain, sparks – have strong generative associations: on the one hand, as fructifying agents, they are analogous to sperm; on the other, flowers are feminine in their associations of beauty, perfume, delicacy, and so on. Flowers are, after all, the sexual organs of plants, both male and female, and this explains why traditionally they are symbols of regeneration and as such are closely allied to the mysteries of transformation and death, as in the well-known seventeenth century poems 'Life' and 'Vertue' by George Herbert (another Welshman), in the second of which he addresses a rose, reminding it that: "Thy root is ever in its grave, / And thou must die",[13] or as in Pasternak's description of Yuri's coffin in *Dr. Zhivago*:

> He was surrounded by a great many flowers, whole bushes of white lilac, hard to find at this season, cyclamens and cineraria in pots and baskets. The flowers screened the light from the windows. The light filtered thinly through the banked flowers to the face and hands of the corpse and the wood and the lining of the coffin. Shadows lay on the table in a pattern of leaves and branches as if they had only just stopped swaying.
>
> . . . In these hours when the silence, unfilled by any ceremony, was made almost tangibly oppressive by a sense of absence, only the flowers took the place of the singing and the psalms.
>
> They did more than blossom and smell sweet. In unison, like a choir, perhaps hastening decomposition, they unstintingly poured out their fragrance and, imparting something of their scented strength to everyone, seemed to be accomplishing a ritual.
>
> The kingdom of plants can easily be thought of as the nearest neighbour to the kingdom of death. *Perhaps the mysteries of transformation and the enigmas of life which so torment us are concentrated in the green of the earth, among the trees in graveyards and the flowering shoots springing from their beds.* Mary Magdalene, not at once recognising Jesus risen from the grave, took Him for the gardener. (Italics mine, R.B.)[14]

Once again, then, we are dealing with symbols of transformation. Flowers, whether rooted in skulls or simply wafting across the sky, are redemptive, organic agents of new life in the garden of paradise. They tumble from the page as the poet writes on it, or they grow out of his pen, and they turn into clouds which themselves have powerful symbolic meanings, suggesting both the constantly changing veil which is drawn over the phenomenal world and the life-cycle itself: rain, water, fecundity, growth, metamorphosis. Clouds occur in seventeen of the forty drawings in *DPDT*, always as agents of change.[15] In the Cabbalah, the cloud is one of the symbols of God's glory (the same 'Glory' which re-emerges in Christian tradition along with the 'Power' and the 'Kingdom' in The Lord's Prayer): it is an element in the secret spelling of the one name of the divinity which in Judaism is feminine in gender, the *Shekhinah* – that which is both hidden and manifest.[16] And in Christian tradition, Jesus too was taken up into a cloud, which in gnostic, esoteric terms is to say that he merged with the *Shekhinah*, the ouranic mother goddess who is the Queen of Heaven, throned in the fire of the sun: a theme which is embedded in the symbolism of Richards's drawing of horses and clouds for 'Fern Hill' (fig. *29*), as we shall see in Chapter V. Flowers, clouds, winged birds and flames are all connected syntactically as well as semantically in the deep stuctures of the language of symbolism; and both Thomas and Richards spoke that language fluently. We are reminded that 'anthology' means 'flower-sayings' or 'word-bouquet' (from ἄνθος meaning 'flower' and λόγος meaning 'word'), and this is itself an apt comment on *DPDT*. And could it be that the blossoms in Richards's drawings are from apple-trees, as in Thomas's lines in the late poem 'In country sleep', where he describes the visitation of "the Thief meek as the dew" to the holy and paradisal dream-country inhabited by the girl, presumably his lover, who lies asleep beside him, beneath the clouds and on a carpet of flowers? (See fig. 31)

> This night and each night since the falling star you were born,
> Ever and ever he finds a way, as the snow falls,
>
> *As the rain falls*, hail on the fleece, as the vale mist rides
> Through the haygold stalls, *as the dew falls on the wind-*
> *Milled dust of the apple tree and the pounded islands*
> *Of the morning leaves, as the star falls, as the winged*
>   *Apple seed glides,*
> *And falls, and flowers in the yawning wound at our sides,*
> As the world falls, silent as the cyclone of silence. (Italics mine, R.B.)[17]

IV

Variants of the Drawings

1 HERONS AND SKULLS : FISHER KING AND GRAAL

The Enitharmon Press edition of *DPDT* reproduces one of four copies of
Thomas's *Collected Poems* which Ceri Richards is known to have made
drawings in, in the late autumn or winter of 1953. It is helpful to our
understanding of both Richards's artistic methods and his symbolism to
compare the three of these versions which are available.

DPDT contains forty pages of drawings, excluding the cover-design (fig.
1). The Swansea Central Library version contains thirty-six drawings and
also has a cover design. Just as for *DPDT*, the front has a semi-profile
portrait of Thomas holding a quill, from which grow flowers. On the back,
instead of two lovers embracing against a background of sea, hills and
wheeling gulls, there is a heron standing in water, with clouds and a hill
behind: an alternative version of the design for 'Over Sir John's Hill' in
DPDT (fig. 21), except that in the Swansea version the heron faces right
instead of left. The third version, which Richards gave to his sister, Mrs.
Esther Thomas, and her husband, contains twenty illustrated pages but no
cover-design. The fourth copy, which he gave to the Hon. Mrs. Lucille
Frost, has unfortunately been lost or mislaid, and must be discounted from
this discussion.[1]

Frances Richards also has a spare copy of a cover-design (fig. 20) which
possibly belongs by rights with Mrs. Thomas's version. Here, the heron is
also used as a motif, but rather than replacing the lovers on the back as in the
Swansea version, it appears on the front, replacing the semi-profile of the
poet, and is nearly identical to the design for 'Over Sir John's Hill' in
DPDT. The back-cover sketch takes up several motifs which Richards
explored in various combinations in *DPDT*, for example, on the front cover
(fig. 1), and for poems like 'On no work of words' (fig. 30), the 'Author's
Prologue' (fig. 6) and 'This bread I break' (fig. 17) – with its ink-bottle,

quill, table-top and handwritten sheets of paper on which a skull perches, and its plant-stem growing out of the skull's eye-sockets and flowering into a sky strewn with clouds and gulls. As on the front cover of *DPDT*, the quill is symbolically identified with leaves and associated with flames (a reading further supported by the last drawing in *DPDT*[2]), and ink is connected with the sacrificial imagery of blood and wine, while flowers merge with clouds, as fragile symbols of metamorphosis and transience, as in many other drawings in *DPDT*. And, by the very fact of its substitution for the two different images on the other cover-designs (and here the order of composition is immatieral), the heron with its feet in the water becomes identified both with "the lovers, their arms / Round the griefs of the ages" and also *with the poet himself*. This identification is hinted at in 'Over Sir John's Hill', where Thomas sees himself and the heron as singing companions: "The heron and I, / I young Aesop fabling to the near night by the dingle / Of eels, saint heron hymning in the shell-hung distant / Crystal harbour vale", and also in the lines in the same poem: "the heron, ankling the scaly / Lowlands of the waves / Makes all the music."[3] The connection is clarified in images recurring in other poems. In 'Poem on his birthday' for example, we find "Herons spire and spear", "Herons, steeple stemmed, bless", "Herons walk in their shroud", and, most interesting of all, "druid herons' vows";[4] while in 'Poem in October', Thomas speaks of "the heron / Priested shore".[5]

In this way, this handsome, long-legged water bird, with its elegantly phallic head and neck, itself becomes an emblem for spiritual trans-formation through both poetry and erotic love. In so doing, it partakes of the symbolism that is traditionally associated with many birds: it is as 'blithe' as Shelley's skylark, as 'immortal' as Keats's nightingale, as 'free' as the swallow in the folk song 'Donna Donna', and so on. But it also has more specific associations, shared by Thomas and Richards from their boyhoods in Wales. First of all, it is a hunter, a fisher, with a beak that is a 'spear', and this motif is picked up by Richards in a drawing on the small title-page of both Mrs. Thomas's and the Swansea versions (fig. 22, reproduced from the latter), which is unillustrated in *DPDT*. Here, the words 'COLLECTED POEMS' are contained within a fish which a heron holds in its mouth, having just plucked it from beneath the waves. As is well known, the fish is an ancient fertility symbol (i.e., of transformation), which also combines the spiritual and the erotic: it is both the phallus and the light which lives and moves secretly in darkness. And as Jean Markale notes in *Women of the Celts*: "The early Christians used the image of the fish not only as a badge of recognition, but also because *Christ represented the eternal food that his message had come to promise, namely a return to the life of paradise.* " (Italics mine, R.B.)[6] One is also reminded of Ted Hughes's fine essay for children, 'Capturing Animals', in which he describes his poem, Pike, as "one of my prize catches", and says of the process of writing itself that: "*This is hunting and the poem is a new species of creature, a new specimen of the life outside your own*", and that: "You will read back through what you have written and you will get a shock. *You will have captured a spirit, a creature.*" (Italics mine, R.B.)[7] So the heron is not only equated with the poet, who captures the poem (a 'spirit' and a 'creature' in its own right, and also "eternal food") by fishing in "the depths of his own inmost nature in order to reach the gnosis", but also symbolises the strange Celtic figure of the Fisher King in the Graal legend. As J. E. Cirlot writes: "Fishing amounts to extracting the unconscious elements from deep-lying sources – the 'elusive' treasure of legend or, in other words, wisdom. To fish for souls is quite simply a matter of knowing how to fish *in* the soul."[8] The goddess Wisdom, $\Sigma o\phi\iota\alpha$, is to be found by looking into the fecund maternal ocean of *one's own subconscious*, while the symbolic connection between herons and lovers suggests that fulfilled sexual love also opens the floodgate to that 'oceanic' sense of bliss and peace in "the life of paradise". These are "the lineaments of gratified desire" which Blake spoke of. Symbolically, the heron, then, is at once the poet (both as 'hymning' singer and musician, and as hunter and fisher); the Fisher King who is keeper and guardian of the sacred and mysterious object which is the goal of the Graal quest; the male or female lover in the genital embrace; and also a 'saint' or 'priest', a 'druid' who 'walks' in his 'shroud' – that is to say, a hierophant, a shaman, the psychopomp who presides over the mysteries of life and death and, in trance, accompanies the souls of the dead on their journey to the other world and then returns to this world.

This series of interpretations is supported further by several other fine works by Richards, in which the heron is once again associated with both death, fertility and poetry, specifically in connection with Dylan Thomas. In the 1954 pen-and-ink drawing entitled *Requiem for Dylan Thomas* (fig. 23), instead of having a fish in its beak, the heron is holding an upturned skull in which sits a bouquet of flowers: clearly a development of the same image we have traced in the *DPDT* drawings for 'And death shall have no

53

dominion' and 'This bread I break'. Here, however, there is an apparently minor but extremely important difference, which must not be overlooked. The skull has been *inverted*, to become a cup, pot or vessel which is unequivocally life-bearing, for death turned upside down *equals* birth, new life and resurrection.[9] In this connection, it is fascinating to refer to Markale again. In his chapter entitled 'The Grail, or the Quest for Woman', through detailed examination of many Celtic sources, he traces *the origin of the Graal vessel itself to a skull*, which was used as a kind of 'chalice' in pre-Christian Celtic ceremonies.[10] This information gives an exciting twist to our interpretation of Richards's drawings, adding a dimension which, whether he was conscious of it or not at the time of composition, is entirely in keeping both with his intention and our foregoing discussion. For thus the flowers of art, love and poetry, blooming immortally in the pot of death overturned, are equated both with the Christ-like fish in fig. 22 (the treasure in the depths of one's unconscious, as is suggested by the dictum "Christ is within you"), and also with the magical, transforming liquid (an 'immortal' love potion?) contained in the Graal vessel. In Richards's 1954 drawing, lines of force beneath the skull make it quite clear that the heron has just lifted the skull out of the waters. Moreover, a stone parapet in the foreground (whose shape is reminiscent of the pile of books in fig. 19) has a shrub in front of it on the left, festooned with shredded scraps of paper tied around it like a ribbon. On these are bits of handwriting, not all of which are legible, but among them can be traced a quotation from the penultimate stanza of Thomas's fine late 'Poem on his birthday':

> ...the closer I move
> To death, one man through his sundered hulks,
>   The louder the sun blooms
> And the tusked, ramshackling sea exults;
>   And every wave of the way
> And gale I tackle, the whole world then,
>   With more triumphant faith
> Than ever was since the world was said,
>   Spins its morning of praise . . .[11]

Here, not only does the sun itself 'bloom' like a flower, but the sea too 'exults' as Thomas goes forward through life into death, 'tackling' both 'waves' and 'gales' exactly like a sea-bird that both sails and swims – and, perhaps also reminding us once again of Dylan Eil Ton in *The Mabinogion* who, "the moment he was baptised... made for the sea. And there and then, as soon as he came to the sea he received the sea's nature, and swam as well as the best fish in the sea". The whole stanza throws out a magnificent challenge to death, defying darkness with light and sound, and culminating in an image which identifies the creation of the world itself with the poetic act of saying. Richards's extraordinarily eloquent drawing matches the poem perfectly, and shows just how deep his reading of Thomas was. So far as I have been able to trace, the first time that images of herons appear in his work is in *DPDT* and its variants, which again demonstrates his indebtedness to Thomas, and also how his images were developed organically over long periods like Thomas's own. The owl-image which becomes dominant later also occurs for the first time in this period (1952-3), always associated with the poet, and the 1955 black and white lithograph *Homage to Dylan Thomas* has a very similar image of a heron with upturned skull and bouquet as in the 1954 drawing, except for the additional presence of an owl (compare figs. 23 and 25); and both herons, skulls and owls reappear ten years later in *The Dylan Thomas Suite* lithographs.[12]

2 TRANSFORMATIONS

The only one of the three known variants which has the exact date of composition recorded in it is *DPDT*. The Swansea version has 'Drawings made in November 1953' in Richards's handwriting, with his signature below, on the page facing the poet's dedication 'To Caitlin'. Mrs. Thomas's version has no date recorded in it, and she cannot remember exactly when her brother made the drawings or when he gave the book to her, although she has written to me that "they were probably done very soon after Dylan's death". This is borne out by Frances Richards's memory of this version having been a Christmas present from her husband to his sister in December 1953. Thus, while we know for sure that all the versions were executed over a short period, it is not possible to ascertain with absolute certainty either the exact order in which they were composed, or whether Richards worked directly from one version to another by copying (possibly even moving from one version to another and back again), or made each series independently from the others. This is a great pity, since information of this kind would have made it possible to draw very precise conclusions about his working methods. It is, however, understandable, since these events happened over a quarter of a century ago, memory fades, and to those close to him, his work on these drawings would have been unremarkable in itself since he was always sketching out ideas for new projects, of which this was merely one among many, and all his family knew that he had already done a lot of work on Dylan Thomas's poems.

Despite this, there is at least some further evidence, both circumstantial and internal, to help us in making tentative assertions about the order in which the various versions were composed. Although we cannot assess the quality of Mrs. Frost's version, and even though she is reported to have said that she thought the drawings in it "twice as good as the poems", Frances Richards believes that it was the first one her husband designed, and that it was not so fully or richly illustrated as *DPDT*. As for the Swansea copy, detailed comparison of the drawings indicates that this too was designed before *DPDT*, as we have already suggested in our discussion of the illustrations for 'The force that through the green fuse drives the flower' in the two versions (figs. 9 and 11). Apart from this, the fact that *DPDT* has the greater number of drawings suggests that it is a later and more elaborated working of an idea, and that the Swansea version is an earlier draft. This is borne out by a number other factors. First, the many identical or nearly identical drawings for the same poem in both versions often show greater elaboration in *DPDT*, particularly in shading, the addition of detail, and the fuller exploitation of the visual potential of an image. This can be seen by comparing the designs in the two editions for 'O make me a mask', 'This bread I break' and 'And death shall have no dominion' (figs. 14-19). In all these cases, a far greater degree of attentiveness and skill is present in the *DPDT* version. In only one case is the Swansea version of an identical drawing slightly more elaborate, in the memory-sketch of Caitlin Thomas on the dedication page, where the shading is heavier. In most other cases, the Matisse-like line-drawings in the two versions are so similar as to be almost identical, with little to choose between them except for subjective preference, although even in these the *DPDT* version is often slightly more worked, as for 'Was there a time' (figs. 12 and 13). For other short poems, as for 'The force that through the green fuse drives the flower', the motif has been changed and clearly improved upon in *DPDT*. Furthermore, *DPDT* has ten pages illustrated which have no drawings at all in the Swansea version,[13] and five of these are among the best in the series. Conversely, there are only four pages illustrated in the Swansea version which do not have drawings in *DPDT*,[14] and the only one of these that is of extra interest is the half-title page (fig. 22), while the images in the others are inferior and not fully appropriate to the poems, as for 'Before I knocked' (fig. 8). For longer poems like the 'Author's Prologue' and the sequence 'Vision and Prayer', the relative states of the accompanying drawings also show a closer and deeper reading of the poems in *DPDT*, as can be seen by comparing figs. 2, 3 and 6 with figs. 4 and 5, in particular the addition of the fine Welsh dragon in fig. 6.

Even if this argument concerning the order of composition cannot be conclusive, it is at least clear from it that, of the three available versions, *DPDT* is the best. And that this was the copy which Richards gave his wife seems entirely appropriate, which is not, of course, to suggest that the others are not also of great interest and value. Quality apart though, what evidence we do have leads me to suggest the following order of composition: first, Mrs. Frost's copy; then the Swansea copy; thirdly, *DPDT*; and lastly, Mrs. Thomas's copy, which (if this is correct) would have been the only one made after Dylan Thomas's death. It is, of course, possible that Mrs. Thomas's version was also an earlier draft; and it is also conceivable that the Swansea version was an afterthought or variation, although for the reasons given above, I do not think this likely to have been the case. Mrs. Thomas's version has no illustrations that do not appear in either *DPDT* or the Swansea version, except for some charming adornments of flower-shapes bordering 'Poem on his birthday', which are entirely appropriate for a Christmas present but of no special artistic interest. I would also hazard the guess that in their original conception neither *DPDT* nor its variants was ever consciously 'intended for publication' – even though that thought may have crossed Richards's mind once he became immersed in the project – but that they were prompted by his need to re-read Thomas's poems more thoroughly, in preparation for the joint public reading and exhibition which the two of them had planned to hold in the Glynn Vivian Gallery in Swansea on Thomas's return from America. As Richards read, he drew. That this project never came to anything is perhaps as much a pity as the fact that Thomas never lived to complete his projected long poem, 'In Country Heaven',[15] or to collaborate with Stravinsky on an opera. But Richards's 'collaboration' with Thomas did not end with the poet's death: if anything, it derived as much strength from it as Shelley did from Keats's or Tennyson did from Hallam's, which gave us, respectively, 'Adonais' and 'In Memoriam'.

One final point emerges from comparison of the different versions: it enables us to trace the outlines of Richards's method of composition and to relate this, firstly, to a statement of his own about it, and secondly, to one by Thomas. Here is Richards, writing in 1963.

> My painting must create a sensation inseparable from the feeling I have for the subject from which it stems. A subject is a necessity, for it presents a renewal of problems and discipline. The chance that the artist encounters when painting and with which he has to struggle, give tension to the work. Working with a greater or lesser struggle images are made and destroyed, until what I hope will happen, happens.
>
> Discovering a subject for a start – which for me means one that haunts me – I make masses of the speediest notes to catch at all sorts of evocations. This foraging is stimulating because the speed of drawing spills out a spate of unpredictable images, matching the pace of time to an intuitive change. I take advantage of all my experiences of events or objects, and to use the observational faculty in the graphism of drawing is of special delight and importance to me.
>
> The object that a painting becomes is the result of a struggle with a technique which implies the use of subtle substances and the continual alteration of images on the more imposing scale of the canvas.
>
> Working through from direct visual facts to a more sensory counterpart of reality of my subject, I hope that as I work I can create later on an intense metaphorical image for my subject.
>
> Temperamentally I feel attuned to the movement and dynamism that lies in nature and events, and in my forms I like to realise this subtlety and complexity.[16]

The process described here in Richards's characteristically modest and down-to-earth manner – discovering a subject as a kind of 'objective correlative', the need for it to be one that 'haunts' him, allowing the subconscious full rein in a 'foraging' for 'evocations' by making 'the speediest' of sketches, and the 'struggle' with the material in 'making' and 'destroying' images – is all extraordinarily well exemplified in the various drafts we have been discussing. Interestingly, his use of the word 'foraging' to describe the process of locating and articulating "a spate of unpredictable images" is not far removed from the ideas of 'hunting' and 'fishing' which we have explored earlier in this chapter. All these are metaphors drawn from the times when humans were hunter-gatherers and, more important, neither forager, fisher nor hunter can ever know in advance exactly what they will find or catch, or where they will find or catch it. Equally interesting is Richards's double emphasis on natural observation and his attempts to integrate what he has seen in the outside world by means of "an intense metaphorical image": that is, on working from "direct visual facts" and transforming these into a symbolic "counterpart of reality". Although he affirms that his work is strongly rooted in all his "experiences of events or objects" and in observation of the outside world – a faculty which he delights in and uses to full advantage – he does not speak of *mimesis* here. Richards perhaps would have agreed with Rebecca West that: "A copy of the universe is not what is required of art; one of the damned thing is ample." His concern is not to copy but to 'realise' and transform what he sees into "an intense metaphorical image". Transformation, then, is the key not just to his form but also to his content: his technique itself consists of transforming ("the creation of creating"), and transformation is also the *subject* underlying all his subjects, which is precisely "the movement and dynamism in nature and events" which he feels "temperamentally attuned to". The remarks about 'speed' and the 'unpredictable' content of his images that arise spontaneously during the course of composition, and the "matching the pace of time to an intuitive change", also indicate a developed understanding of the mental processes involved in symbol-formation, which Jung explored in depth in many of his works,[17] and these are also incidentally akin, if not identical, to those discussed in Jung's essay on synchronicity and in his foreword to the *I Ching*.[18] In this respect Richards's remarks about the time factor are especially interesting. His use of the phrase "subtle substances" does not, I think, refer solely to pen and ink or brushes, paint and canvas, but is to be taken as an indication that, like Thomas, he regarded his own working methods as a spiritual discipline, and the artefacts which resulted, as objects endowed with mysterious and possibly magical properties. And perhaps most interesting of all is the similarity of many of these remarks, and of their tenor as a whole, to the well-known statement by Thomas about his own poetic technique, in a letter dated March 23rd 1938:

> ...A poem by myself *needs* a host of images, because its centre is a host of images. I make one image – though 'make' is not the word, I let, perhaps, an image be 'made' emotionally in me and then apply it to what intellectual and critical forces I possess – let it breed another, let that image contradict

the first, make, out of the third image bred out of the other two together, a fourth contradictory image, and let them all, within my imposed formal limits, conflict. *Each image holds within it the seed of its own destruction, and my dialectical method, as I understand it, is a constant building up and breaking down of the images that come out of the central seed, which is itself destructive and constructive at the same time.* (Italics mine, R.B.)[19]

The description differs in details from Richards's, but in all essentials the same process is being outlined: 'letting' an image arise from the sub-conscious, allowing it to proliferate into other images, and consciously struggling with them to integrate them in a single, composite image which is both its own centre and circumference. Richards's comment that: "Working with a greater or lesser struggle images are made and destroyed", is extraordinarily close to the last sentence in Thomas's statement. He may well have known these remarks of Thomas's, and at least partially modelled his own upon them; but even if this was not so, it is further evidence of the unusual kinship of spirit between the two men. It is small wonder, in the light of this, that the poem of Thomas's which Richards returned to most often was 'The force that through the green fuse drives the flower', since it is here that Thomas's "central seed, which is itself destructive and con-structive at the same time" is most directly pushed out of its maternal soil. In the *Black Apple of Gower* series, Richards made (or rather, discovered, or created) the most haunting composite symbol of his whole artistic career, which alone assures him a place among the greatest artists of this century, and is itself an expression of this "central seed" of all transformations in both human civilisation, nature and the cosmos; and it is to this that we now turn.

V

The 'Black Apple of Gower' and its Symbolism

1   APPLE AND MANDALA : THE WATER-COLOUR VERSION

The first of the three major treatments of the *Afal du Brogŵyr* has an interesting history. This was the chalk and water-colour on paper rubbed over wood, dated 1952 and measuring 15" x 22", which Mrs. Lucille Frost gave to C. G. Jung, and is now in the collection belonging to Jung's son in Zurich (fig. 36). On 21 May 1958, Jung wrote to Richards to thank him for the painting, as follows:

> Dear Sir
>
> Mrs. F. has kindly brought me your picture, for which I owe you many thanks. It came as a great surprise to me. I must confess, however, that I have no relation whatever to modern art unless I understand a picture. This is occasionally the case and is also the case with your picture. Purely aesthetically I appreciate the delicacy of the colours. The background (wood) points to matter and thus to the medium in which the round thing is to be found and with which it contrasts. The round thing is one of many. It is astonishingly filled with compressed corruption, abomination and explosiveness. It is pure black substance, which the old alchemists called *nigredo*, that is: blackness, and understood as night, chaos, evil and the essence of corruption, yet the *prima materia* of gold, sun, and eternal incorruptibility. I understand your picture as a confession of the secret of our time.
>
> Many thanks,
>
> Yours sincerely,
>
> C. G. Jung.[1]

This fascinating letter, which goes way beyond mere appreciativeness, poses many questions. Clearly Richards's painting had an immediate and powerful effect on Jung, to have elicited from him such a cryptic and yet precise reply. And what concerned him above all, here as elsewhere, was the

61

work's symbolism or, in his own terminology, its *archetypal* content. It is impossible to say to what extent Richards himself was familiar with or had been directly influenced by Jung's theories at the time this work was composed, but his many mandala-sketches between 1950 and 1952 do indicate that he was involved with the kind of material Jung was working from. At any rate, as we have shown, much of Richards's work was intentionally symbolist, as was his working method.

What Jung says about "pure black substance" not only picks up the symbolism in Richards's title, but is extraordinarily intuitive since, firstly, the colours actually used by the artist were not black, but pastel shades of great 'delicacy'; and secondly, Jung had no way of knowing Richards's other treatments of the theme, particularly the line-drawing for 'I dreamed my genesis' in *DPDT* in which the 'round thing' *is*, literally, black (see front cover). Aside from this, the letter raises other equally fascinating questions. Its language is emotive: "astonishingly filled with compressed corruption, abomination and explosiveness" and "night, chaos, evil and the essence of corruption". This suggests that the painting came as something rather more than the "great surprise" admitted by Jung, and that he was moved and excited by its power, on an emotional level only half disguised by his disclaimer about "having no relation whatever to modern art" and the measured, scholarly tone he adopts. Perhaps even more challenging are the implications of his parting remark about the picture being "a confession of the secret of our time". We can hardly fail to wonder what, precisely, is this mysterious 'secret' the painting 'confesses' – an odd word to use. But before we attempt to confront these questions, many other considerations need to be explored. Firstly, Gerhard Adler's editorial note in Jung's *Letters* contains an equally illuminating statement by Richards himself:

> He gave Jung a chalk and water-colour study for an oil painting entitled "Afal Du Brogŵyr" (Black Apple of Gower) – Gower is a Welsh *seignory* with very old historical connections and figures in the Arthurian romances. According to the communication from R., the picture expresses *"the great richness, the fruitfulness and great cyclic movement of the poems of Dylan Thomas. The circular image... is the metaphor expressing the sombre germinating force of nature – surrounded by the petals of a flower and seated within earth and sea."* (Italics mine, R.B.)[1]

This statement by Richards comes from a letter sent from his home in Edith Grove, on August 2nd 1968, in reply to Dr. Adler's request for some comments on the meaning of the painting. Its full text, which Dr. Adler kindly sent me, is as follows:

Dear Mr. Adler,

Thank you for your letter.

I send you a print of the drawing (chalk and watercolour. 15 x 22 approx) which was in the collection of the late Prof. Jung.

I remember you borrowing the letter which I had from him about it.

The drawing was a study for a painting which I have in my possession. The title of this painting is (in Welsh) 'Black Apple of Gower'. This seems to be a most obtuse sort of title – it is my own title and expresses for me the great richness, the fruitfulness and great cyclic movement and rhythms of the poems of Dylan Thomas. The circular image as in the drawing (in question) is the metaphor expressing the sombre germinating force of nature – surrounded by the petals of a flower, and seated within earth and sea – (badly registered in the print).

Prof. Jung's drawing is capable of many interpretations; and I was proud and interested to have his letter about it. Mrs. Lucille Frost often told me how profoundly interested he was in the significance of the mandala.

I hope you will find this letter helpful.

Yours very sincerely,

Ceri Richards
(born 1903)

Richards's letter is as fascinating as Jung's own. Firstly, his use of the word 'mandala' (a term which Jung made current) suggests that even if he had not familiarised himself with any of Jung's writings in 1952 when these works were composed, he had certainly done so by the time this letter was written. More important, his self-deprecating, somewhat playful admission of the 'obtuseness' of the title, and his teasing refusal to be drawn into saying anything too narrowly specific about the meaning of Jung's water-colour, both clearly point to the symbolist intention behind the work. Critics in their superior fashion, sometimes tend to give the impression that poets and artists "do not know what they are doing" simply because they work intuitively. This letter makes it abundantly clear that Richards's understanding of symbolism was profound in both artistic and psychological terms. He knew full well that symbols can never simply mean one thing, but are always "capable of many interpretations". A symbolistic interpretation of the *Afal du Brogŵyr* series is therefore all the more justified. As for the "very old historical connections" between Gower and the Arthurian romances which Dr. Adler points to, although the extent of Richards's knowledge of these is unclear, we do know from independent sources that he was familiar with *The Mabinogion*. His elder daughter, Mrs. Rachel Patterson, has told me that he used to read her stories from it when she was small, in Lady Charlotte Guest's translation.

Most important of all, however, is the insight Richards's letter gives us not only into the fact of there being a deep connection between the *Afal du Brogŵyr* series and Dylan Thomas's poems, but into the precise nature of what he took to be their central theme: above all: "the great richness, the fruitfulness and great cyclic movement and rhythms" as metaphors of "the sombre germinating force of nature". Here, the artist's own statement shows beyond doubt that we are dealing with the same dominant motif which we have traced in all the other works so far discussed: the life-cycle, of which the work of a poet or an artist is at once a part, a recognition, a metaphor, a celebration and a creative continuation – in short, transformation itself. And in this light, for all its esoteric, alchemical terms, Jung's letter expresses exactly the same principle: the struggle between life and death, light and darkness, etc., within this process. Now if we put the two statements by Richards and Jung together, the painting becomes entirely legible. We can read it as though the circular shape were a kind of transverse section of "the force that through the green fuse drives the flower" – as though we were looking down from above, through flower and stem, into the dark root of poetic or artistic inspiration itself. And as Jung's emphasis on "night, chaos, evil" etc. suggests, what we find in those depths might well be as potent, mysterious and frightening as the eerie death's head out of whose eye sockets grow the same plants of art and poetry which we have traced in other drawings.

Yet there is also another aspect to the picture. The petals of the flower that surround "the round thing" and blend organically into the markings of the wood grain (whose lines suggest both the deep currents of the sea and the strata beneath the earth, as well as organic matter) are also identifiable with the rays of the sun, reminding us of the image of the sun 'blooming' in 'Poem on his Birthday', as if the 'apple' or 'mandala' itself were spreading its light in the submarine or subterranean darkness of the unconscious: like the fish in the heron's mouth; or a diamond embedded in ore waiting to be discovered by a prospector; or the alchemical *lapis philosophorum* within the *nigredo* or *prima materia*; or, perhaps, even like death itself in a well-known poem by Henry Vaughan:

> Dear beauteous death! The Jewel of the Just
>   Shining nowhere but in the dark;
> What mysteries do lie beyond thy dust;
>   Could man outlook that mark![2]

So, for all its aesthetic delicacy of tone and form, the painting is ambiguous. And this ambiguity is no mere manneristic decoration: the work is paradoxical at a deep psychic level, right in the 'core' or 'grain' of its meaning or, rather, meanings. Moreover, the precise, considered quality of Richards's reply to Adler, ten years or so after the composition of these works, also suggests that the *Afal du Brogwyr* represents and is intended to be read as one of his major syntheses of what Dylan Thomas's work meant for him. The theme of this painting and of the other works like it is therefore central to establishing a complete understanding of Richards's complex relationship with Thomas's poems and, as such, must be seen as the key to the *DPDT* drawings. Therefore, to work out as fully as we can exactly what is going on in the *Afal du Brogwyr* series must be the remaining task of this monograph. But it must be remembered that we are dealing here with a symbol charged with numinosity, so that the task of unravelling its meanings is fraught with difficulties, although the challenge to explore these as fully as possible is equally strong, particularly in the context of the last sentence in Jung's letter.

2 APPLE AND WOMB : THE OIL-PAINTING

The second work in this series is in my view the major masterpiece of Richards's whole artistic career and, by any account, is a striking and unusual picture. This is an oil-painting, measuring 40″ x 30″ (fig. 39), which is in the private London collection of Richards's elder daughter and her husband, Rachel and Colin Patterson. Once again, the connection between the painting and the work of Dylan Thomas is immediately clear: at the bottom of the picture, Richards has inscribed the title – 'AFAL DU BROGWYR', the date – '52, his signature, and also the words *'Gwrogaeth i Dylan Thomas'* ('Homage to Dylan Thomas'). Here, the dark circular shape of the 'apple' is planted in the middle of the Gower Peninsula, Thomas's and Richards's birthplace; and, although this is barely discernible even in the original, let alone in a much smaller photograph, the sentence "The force that through the green fuse drives the flower drives my green age" is faintly scratched in capital letters into the black circle just inside its lower rim. To the right and below the peninsula, the sea stretches around beaches of bright yellow sand, inlets, bays and cliffs; while, behind a sharply defined edge of land and sea, a red sun appears, banded both half way through and at its rim by two thin semi-circular lines of equally bright yellow, its whole image as bold as a work by Blake or Samuel Palmer and expressing a similar luminous, visionary quality. The sky itself consists of horizontal bands of yellow, red and blue, in varying alternations and thicknesses, which suggest both rapid transformations of colour as at sunrise or sunset, and also other colours between them: gold, orange and green. At the top of the picture there is a solid band of black, through which a whitish moon, tinged with blue and banded at its rim with yellow, nearly touches the sun. As Mrs. Patterson has pointed out to me, the geographical position of the sun over the peninsula is neither in the exact East nor West, and it is therefore a moot point whether we are to take it that the morning sun is pushing the tired moon out of the sky or the rising moon is pushing the setting sun on its nightly journey beneath the earth. Is day defeating night, light overcoming darkness, life conquering death, or vice-versa? I would suggest that both interpretations are valid and the image is complex and ambivalent in every possible way, and yet in its very ambivalence it makes a powerful and meaningful statement about the opposition and complementation of these forces within both the natural cycle and the transformative work of the poet and the artist.

The use of perspective is also richly ambivalent, and the painting demands to be looked at in two distinct ways simultaneously. As in the water-colour, the viewer is invited to look down, vertically, at the 'round thing', as though it were either a hole in the earth, like a well or a pothole, or a growth out of it; and this 'aerial photographic' effect is confirmed by the map-like contours of the Gower coast which surround the central shape. But the perspective is equally to be taken as horizontal, an impression which has been deliberately worked for by Richards both in his use of colour and in the way that both sun and moon at once echo and contrast with the 'apple'. The rocks which surround the apple present an overall grey impression, of varying intensity, and are worked in flecks of black and white. But just above the apple, this gives way to green patched with gold, indicating the sun's imprint on grassy hills and sand-dunes. This presents the unmistakeable picture of a cross-section of the earth's geological strata, seen, as it were, sideways. By this reading, the 'apple' appears as a thing *under* the earth, embedded in rock, pushing into the topsoil, and reaching *upwards* through these layers towards the surface and sunlight, once again, like a plant. This upward movement is emphasised formally by the presence of the sun directly above and behind the 'apple', and by the fact that its perimeter has exactly the same dimensions as that of the apple, though it contrasts with it in colour. The apple is thus both a 'mate' and a 'reflection' of the sun – its complement and enantiomorph within the earth itself: "as above, so below". The sun-like associations of the flower-petals in Jung's mandala study have now become quite explicit: just as the radiant red and yellow sun rules over the heavens, so the 'black sun' of the apple reigns in the underworld.

Personally, I find that my natural tendency in looking at this extraordinary painting is for the eyes to move upwards, simply because of the way in which the celestial sun is positioned immediately above and behind the buried sun, like an aura or halo; and for this reason I prefer to think that the painting depicts sunrise and morning rather than sunset and evening – that is to say, that its emphasis is on creation, fecundity and growth rather than on destruction, disintegration and death – and this reading is supported by Richards's comments to Gerhard Adler that the "circular image" in Jung's version expresses "the germinating force of nature". Even so, he did use the word 'sombre' to describe this process, and we have only to return to the first stanza of 'The force that through the green fuse drives the flower' and to Richards's drawing for the poem in *DPDT* to remember that *the creative force and the destructive force are one and the same*. They are simply the twin 'faces' of the single mystery of transformation, since "the road up and the road down is one and the same" (Heracleitus).[3] Hence, whether one's personal predilection in interpreting the direction of the energy-flow in this painting is upwards or downwards, either reading must inevitably contain and include its own opposite. And that Richards intended this to be so is made explicit in the presence of the moon at the top of the picture, which contrasts not only with the sun it touches, but also with the 'apple' itself. The dark sky around the moon is, to say the least, ominous. For these reasons, the central image of the apple itself might be said *to contain elements of both sun and moon*, that is, of both day and night, light and darkness, life and death, and so on, not to mention the sexual symbolism which has been attached by every human culture throughout the centuries to sun and moon, irrespective of whether the sun is regarded as masculine and the moon feminine (as in most of our patriarchal cultures), or vice-versa (as in certain cultures like the Celtic ones, in which traces of a previous gynaeocracy have not been totally eradicated, and feminine sun-deities not entirely overthrown by masculine ones of the Sumerian Marduk or Greek Apollo type). It is also obvious that the swirling fig-like forms within the 'apple' itself are explicit sexual and generative images with both masculine and feminine connotations; and the apple can therefore also be interpreted as the primordial, chthonic 'womb' which gives birth to both sun and moon, son and daughter, or – if one prefers – daughter and son. And although masculine elements are undeniably present, in shapes which suggest testicles and possibly also sperm, the predominant symbolism in the interior of the 'apple' is feminine, as I hope to show conclusively by tracing in more depth and detail its mythical associations, as well as its origins in Richards's personal artistic development.

But first, we also have some equally illuminating comments about the works in this series from Frances Richards to offset the statements by her husband and Jung. These remarks are recorded from an interview I made with her at her house in Barnes in June 1977:

> Mrs. Frost bought the water-colour version as a present for Jung. She was his patient and knew Jung very well. What Jung did seem to understand was some of the symbolism. But I'm not sure that he was entirely right about it, and I don't think that Ceri had quite the same idea as Jung... The big oil painting is a very fine work. It doesn't derive from any one *specific* story in Welsh mythology, though the shape in the middle is symbolic and so are the things inside it that look like the core and the pips. There's a lot of symbolism in it but much of this is very personal... *As for the meaning, I'll tell you what I think. I think it depicts the centre of the fruit and also the centre of the interior of the earth. And it's also the beginning of things, of the fruit. That's what I think that big round black shape is. And it's got the Gower coast around it, and the sea.* (Italics mine, R.B.)

As far as the first part of this statement is concerned, with respect, it must be pointed out that it does not matter at all that Richards's idea was different from that of Jung or that his symbolism was 'personal' (i.e., that

he had evolved the symbol through a long process of interior exploration
and formal experiment). When symbolism in a work of art communicates
itself effectively, this is usually the case. And its very communicability
necessarily implies that the symbolism operates on a social, i.e. collective,
level, and not merely on a private one. A symbol in a work of art is never
merely personal, although it operates on different individuals in an emotive
and subjective way which varies in intensity and in meaningfulness from
one person to another. Nor does a symbol in a work of art ever have just *one*
meaning: it is never a simple 'pointer' either operating at a mere intellectual
level or capable of being ticked off as in an equation in which *signifiant* and
signifié balance and cancel each other out perfectly. It is wise, of course,
when considering symbolism, to remember I. A. Richards's insistence on
'correctness' of interpretation, and the necessary role played by the intellect
in sorting between admissible and inadmissible readings; since, if the
intellect did not perform this function, any symbol could mean anything
one liked: it could bear an *infinite* number of interpretations, based on any
whim or prejudice, a situation which would reduce any concept of meaning
to chaos and absurdity, since a meaning is of necessity both limited and
limiting, and selectively determined and determining, by very virtue of
excluding other meanings. From the opposite pole, it could be (and has
been) argued, equally absurdly, that, strictly speaking, a symbol 'means'
nothing, because it is always itself and none other than itself. As Gertrude
Stein put it: "A rose is a rose is a rose." But while such a view may be a
healthy corrective to the wilder or more abstruse tendencies in symbolic
interpretation which may sometimes occur (for example during the
decadence of an artistic or literary movement), without a symbol's pointing
in some direction outside itself there could be no meanings at all. The Greek
δύμβολον means 'a token, pledge or sign by which one infers something',
and δυμβαλλειν means 'to bring together, compare, infer' (from δυν- or
δυμ- meaning 'together' and βάλλειν meaning 'to throw').

The signifying potential of a symbol in a work of art is always multivalent,
ambiguous and syncretistic: i.e., it means no one thing, but a large (though
not infinite) number of meanings, or rather associations, may be read
correctly into it and out of it, in layer on layer, in a manner which is
proliferative in exactly the same way as Thomas's statement about his own
method of poetic composition discussed above: "within. . . imposed formal
limits...a constant building up and breaking down of the images that come

out of the central seed, which is destructive and creative at the same time". Moreover, as the etymology indicates in the idea of 'throwing together', this process operates in art and poetry, as in life, primarily through what Wordsworth in *The Prelude* called the "observation of affinities / In objects where no brotherhood exists / To passive minds";[4] and it is always charged with a deep personal and emotional energy current. This is to say that it works by the registration of *analogy* between at least one pair of the common attributes of two or more entities, through simile, and the merging and identification of such attributes, through metaphor; and this involves the transference of attributes from one entity to another and back again. It also involves a concomitant process of constant accretion and shifting of attributes between entities, which can produce both ambiguity and the extension or diminuition of attributes for any particular entity, with the result that their meanings may change entirely and often even turn into their own opposites. To perceive analogy is exciting: it involves discovery. It is both heuristic and creative; and, at a deep level of thinking, the perception of relatedness between disparate phenomena presupposes belief in a coherent and identifiable order running through all things, irrespective of whether this is consciously affirmed or denied by the artist himself or herself. And this in part explains why great works of art (which are always open to symbolic interpretation) are both universal and also constantly have to be reinterpreted. Beneath this deep level of thinking lie what Jung calls "the archetypes of the collective unconscious", which we all share; and when these gradually surface into consciousness, the images through which they find expression are symbols. In this context, Jung's remarks in 'On the Relation of Analytical Psychology to Poetry' are much to the point here:

> *The creative process, so far as we are able to follow it at all, consists in the unconscious activation of an archetypal image, and in elaborating and shaping this image into the finished work. By giving it shape, the artist translates it into the language of the present, and so makes it possible for us to find our way back to the deepest springs of life.* Therein lies the social significance of art: it is constantly at work educating the spirit of the age, conjuring up the forms in which the age is most lacking. *The unsatisfied yearning of the artist reaches back to the primordial image in the unconscious which is best fitted to compensate for the inadequacy and one-sidedness of the present.* The artist seizes on this image, and in raising it from deepest unconsciousness he brings it into relation with conscious values, thereby transferring it until it can be accepted by the minds of his contemporaries according to their powers. (Italics mine, R.B.)[5]

70

Here Jung's phrase "the deepest springs of life" tallies perfectly with Frances Richards's perception of both "the centre of the interior of the earth" and "the beginning of things" in her husband's painting, as well as with Neumann's "beginning of time: the creation of the world", Thomas's "central seed, which is destructive and constructive at the same time", and Ceri Richards's "sombre germinating force of nature". In different ways, they are all talking about the same thing: transformation, "the creation of creating", and all of this supports our interpretation of the 'apple' as a "primordial image" of the 'womb' in which this process originates and takes place. But all metaphors flow both ways: if the 'black sun' is a subterranean or subaqueous 'womb', it follows according to the processes of analogical thinking which give rise to all metaphor that the celestial sun too should have the connotations of a 'womb in the sky'. This is an important point, crucial to our interpretation, to which we shall return.

3   WOMB AND SUN : THE PEN-AND-INK DRAWING

The symbolic identification of 'apple' and 'womb' is confirmed even more strikingly by the third work in the *Afal du Brogŵyr* series, the *DPDT* drawing which accompanies Thomas's poem 'I dreamed my genesis' (reproduced on the front cover). As its title indicates, the theme of this poem is precisely "the beginning of things", and its last stanza is particularly interesting.

> I dreamed my genesis in sweat of death, fallen
> Twice in the feeding sea, grown
> Stale of Adam's brine until, vision
> Of new man strength, I seek the sun.

These complex, ambiguous lines not only suggest that the poet is dreaming of his own birth in death itself (again linking with Richards's image of the flower rooted in a skull) but, echoing John Donne's tremendous sermon about mortality and "a better resurrection",[6] they contain a global vision of the new Adam Kadmon arising out of baptismal immersion in the sea of his "second death" through the transformative work of poetic and artistic creativity. Once again, the movement is upwards, from the unconscious and unreflecting darkness of 'death' (Jung's *nigredo*), through dream, to the spiritual regeneration, radiance and clarity epitomised by the sun. We have already discussed Thomas's predilection for sun-images in Chapter II, and have noted the presence of suns in Richards's drawings in our discussion of his various uses of the circular form. Here, once again, form and content cannot be separated, and each of Richards's suns in the *DPDT* series is an articulate and appropriate response to corresponding themes in the poems themselves. There is the fireball which rounds off the poem 'Deaths and Entrances' (fig. 34), which, as the title implies, also deals with ends and beginnings, genesis and apocalypse; the sun over hills and sea for 'Poem in October' (fig. 33), and the sun accompanied by forked lightning for one of the hourglass-shaped poems in 'Vision and Prayer' (fig. 35). Perhaps most interesting of these is the drawing for the poem 'Twenty-four years' (fig. 32), in which the chubby figure of the poet on his craggy Welsh hillside looks out longingly across the sea at "the meat-eating sun", which hovers like a halo directly above his head. The sun in this poem is symbolically "meat-eating", I suggest, for at least three reasons. Firstly, it is the heavenly journey's end after death, the Ithaca yearned for by the traveller which can be attained only when life's Odyssey has come full circle, and as such it is a paradisal symbol. Secondly, it is the transformer of natural creative energy on the raw physical level into spiritual power. And, thirdly, it is the celestial 'womb' or 'vagina' of the paradisal female which 'devours' the phallic 'meat' of the mortal male. The point to be emphasised here is that even without reference to the womb-like characteristics of the 'black apple' or 'black sun', the celestial sun is capable of being interpreted as a symbol of femininity in its own right. The context of this image of "the meat-eating sun" in Thomas's lines, which also echo the image of the "shroud sail"[7] in 'The force that through the green fuse drives the flower', bears out this sexual interpretation of the sun symbol:

> In the groin of the natural doorway I crouched like a tailor
> Sewing a shroud for a journey
> By the light of the meat-eating sun.[8]

"The groin of the natural doorway" can be none other than the vagina, the gateway to and from the womb, symbolising also both entry to and exit from the created, physical world. And the 'black apple' too, I suggest, is precisely this "natural doorway", while the sea-journey underlying the images of the 'shroud' and 'shroud sail' is both that of life itself and the voyage from this life to the other world, which Yeats makes across "That dolphin-torn, that gong-tormented sea" towards resurrection in 'Byzantium',[9] and Tennyson also contemplates in his fine late poem 'Crossing the Bar':

> Sunset and evening star,
>   And one clear call for me!
> And may there be no moaning of the bar
>   When I put out to sea...[10]

We have already seen how Thomas's 'Poem on his birthday' ends similarly with he line: "As I sail out to die". The sun seen across the sea, then, is a symbol both of death itself and paradise after death, or of orgasm (the little death) and repose after orgasm; peaceful sleep in a state of prelapsarian innocence in the Garden of Eden: attainment of "the deepest springs of life" and "the beginning of things" in one. All of this is to say that it is also an image of rebirth through death.

To return to 'I dreamed my genesis', here too the images in the last stanza are all strongly erotic: "sweat of death", "the feeding sea" and "Adam's brine" suggest both copulation and orgasm, the nurturing and also hungrily receptive womb, and sperm and female sexual juices. We are reminded that the name of Aphrodite herself, goddess of fertility and erotic love, means 'Born of Sea Foam'. In the penultimate stanza of the poem Thomas also says, "And power was contagious in my birth",[11] and this also reminds us of the image of the "infant-bearing sea" in 'Ceremony After a Fire Raid'.[12] The power he is speaking of is at once instinctual, through the sexual act, and also cultural, through the creation of poetry. The physical and spiritual, the bestial and human, the natural and the civilised, are all united in both acts. Elsewhere, in a letter written in 1953, Thomas connects the sexual and poetic 'acts of creation' explicitly:

> Poetry, heavy in tare though nimble, should be as orgastic and organic as copulation, dividing and unifying, personal but not private, propagating the individual in the mass and the mass in the individual... Man should be two-tooled, and a poet's middle leg is his pencil.[13]

There is certainly no ambiguity here, and, to follow the image through, if "the poet's middle leg is his pencil" (which is etymologically correct: the word 'pencil' derives from the dog Latin word *penecillus* meaning 'little tail' or 'little penis'), then the words which his 'pencil' writes are also a kind of 'spiritual sperm', capable of 'fertilising' the receptive womb-like consciousness of the reader. We are back again with the "winged seeds" of Shelley's 'Ode to the West Wind', and with the blossoms which pour from the poet's pen and page in Richards's drawings. In the light of all this, it would not be surprising if in the sea-and sun-imagery of 'I dreamed my genesis', Thomas was again hinting, obliquely but deliberately, at the etymology of his own name in the story of 'Math Son of Mathonwy' in *The Mabinogion*: 'Sea Son of the Wave', i.e., bearer of the seeds of both life, erotic love and a higher spirituality out of the sea of unconsciousness, brought to the land of life itself only to return eventually to the paradisal womb of the sun. And, furthermore, if the poet's pencil is equated symbolically with the phallus, the 'wound' that Thomas often speaks of in his poems (e.g. "Throw wide to the wind the gates of the wandering boat / For my voyage to begin to the end of my wound" in 'Lie Still, Sleep Becalmed'[14]) may well also be connected symbolically with the wound of the Fisher King, who has been pierced in the thigh and so rendered impotent. And here, just as physical blindness is often the outer vestment of an unusually sharpened spiritual 'in-sight' (embodied clearly in the myth of Teiresias, the blind seer), so the physical (i.e., worldly, social, and perhaps even literally sexual) impotence of the Fisher King may well indicate heightened 'potency' at a spiritual level. And if, as we have suggested in our interpretation of the symbolism of the heron in both Thomas's poems and Richards's drawings, the figures of the Fisher King and the poet are to be identified, and, furthermore, if the Graal vessel itself which the Fisher King guards is an upturned skull, then it follows that the keeper of the secrets of life and death (i.e., of the mysteries of transformation) is none other than the poet too – the degree of his or her 'spiritual potency' even being measurable in direct proportion to his or her 'temporal impotence'. This correlation perhaps gives us a fresh angle on Shelley's dictum at the end of *A Defence of Poetry*, that "Poets are the unacknowledged legislators of the world."

4 SUN GODS AND GODDESSES, HORSES AND CHARIOTS

As for the 'black sun' itself, this is no mere figment of Richards's personal fantasy either. It occurs widely and as a well attested symbol of transformation as far back as the Egyptians. Interestingly, according to

Jung, the 'black sun' is also synonymous with the alchemical *nigredo* and, so he says, is also "roughly the equivalent of what I call the collective unconscious".[15] Small wonder, then, that he was 'surprised' by Richards's painting, if through it he found himself staring into the dark face of the collective unconscious itself! It is possible, however, to be more specific than this. Cirlot writes:

> Now, having established the principal terms of solar symbolism – as an heroic image (*Sol invictus, Sol salutis, Sol iustitiae*), as the divine eye, the active principle and the source of life and energy – let us come back to the dualism of the Sun as regards its hidden passage – its 'Night Sea-Crossing' – symbolic of immanence (like the colour black) and also of sin, occultation and expiation. In the *Rigveda* – Eliade reminds us – *the Sun is ambivalent: on the one hand it is 'resplendent' and on the other it is 'black' or invisible, in which case it is associated with chthonian and funereal animals such as the horse and the serpent.* Alchemists took up this image of the *Sol niger* to symbolise 'prime matter', or the unconscious in its base, 'unworked' state. In other words, the Sun is then at the nadir, in the depths out of which it must, slowly and painfully, ascend towards its zenith. This inevitable ascent does not relate to its daily journey, although this is used as an image, and hence it is symbolised by the transmutation of prime matter into gold, passing through the red and white stages, like the Sun itself in orbit. (Italics mine, R.B.)[16]

Apart from the fact that the whole of this passage supports Jung's alchemical interpretation of Richards's water-colour, the parts of it I have italicised can also be read as a direct commentary on all the works in this series. The 'black sun' or 'apple' is the core of transformation itself, the very zone in which life in all its myriad forms continuously confronts death and grows out of it. Cirlot's mention of the connection between the sun and the horse is interesting too, since the image of the horse also occurs in Richards's drawing for 'Fern Hill' (fig. 29) where it is associated, not with funereal elements as such, but with life in a state of innocent bliss, where a perfect sun shines over a green paradise, as on the first morning of Creation which is depicted in Thomas's lines in that poem:

>   ... it was all
> Shining, it was Adam and maiden,
>   The sky gathered again
> And the sun grew round that very day.
> So it must have been after the birth of the simple light
> In the first, spinning place, the spellbound horses walking warm

Out of the whinnying green stable
On to the fields of praise.[17]

These lines make the connection between horse and sun quite explicitly. And the horses in Richards's drawing too, with their billowing forms and gentle, 'phallic-shaped' necks and heads, seem to be made of the stuff of the clouds which surround them (perhaps also with a hint of sea-foam), and could well be interpreted as the sky-riding steeds that pull the sun's golden chariot. This obvious point seems to have been missed by Cirlot, but is developed interestingly by Markale in his analysis of the Tristan and Iseult legend:

> Mark (or March, a name meaning "horse") is the literary development of the driver of that ritual object of the Bronze Age, the sun chariot; he leads the sun into darkness and delays its rebirth, the usual role of the horse god who is his source.[18]

However, Cirlot does point out that:

> Jung came to wonder if the horse might not be a symbol for the mother, and he does not hesitate to assert that is expresses the magic side of Man, 'the mother within us', that is, intuitive understanding.[19]

Even so, like most writers, Cirlot unquestioningly accepts the conventional patriarchal view that because the sun is 'active' and the earth 'receptive', the former is best fitted with a masculine image and the latter with a feminine one, despite the fact that he describes the sun as "the source of life", a phrase which could equally well suggest femininity in its nurturing aspects. The masculine aspect of the sun is, of course, undeniable since the mythologies of the world are spattered everywhere with sun-gods and heroes. Accordingly, Cirlot reminds us that:

> The idea of the invincible character of the Sun is reinforced by the belief that whereas the Moon must suffer fragmentation (since it wanes) before it can reach its monthly stage of three-day disappearance, the Sun does not need to die in order to descend into hell; it can reach the ocean or lake of the Lower Waters and cross it without being dissolved. *Hence, the death of the Sun necessarily implies the idea of resurrection and actually comes to be regarded as a death which is not a true death.* ...The sudden disappearance of the Sun below the horizon is related to the sudden death of heroes such as Samson, Hercules and Siegfried. (Italics mine, R.B.)[20]

If the sun in the large *Afal du Brogŵyr* oil painting is to be interpreted as setting rather than rising, these comments seem apt enough. Perhaps, to

76

Richards, Thomas *was* a kind of 'sun hero'. However improbable this may sound in literal terms, there is certainly some symbolic truth in it, since, as we have seen, the sun-images which abound in Thomas's poems are nearly always intimately connected to his idea of his own life-pattern and destiny. Even so, the notion of a sun that is wholly masculine, with no ambivalence of gender whatever in its symbolic associations, is highly suspect, because all symbols are inherently capable of transforming their 'values' – or, to use a linguistic term, their 'markedness' – including gender, into their opposites. As Helmut Wilhelm points out in *Change, Eight Lectures on the 'I Ching'*, in ancient Chinese thought there is even "an extremely early tradition that *the earth or at least its product is masculine*; later this conception turned into almost its opposite". (Italics mine, R.B.).[21] And even if the celestial sun were to be regarded as completely masculine, it would still seem right, according to the laws of polarity which regulate all such images, that the black chthonic sun should be regarded as feminine.

The interdependence of all complementary masculine and feminine symbols and the innumerable ways in which both are capable of changing into the other, are well understood by Jung, and his remarks in a chapter of *Symbols of Transformation* entitled 'Symbols of the Mother and of Rebirth' are relevant to the *Afal du Brogŵyr*:

> *The idea of the soil as feminine also embraces the idea of continuous co-habitation with the woman, a physical interpenetration.* The god Shiva, as Mahadeva and Parvati, is both male and female: he has even given one half of his body to his wife Parvati as a dwelling-place. The motif of *continuous cohabitation* is expressed in the well-known lingam symbol found everywhere in Indian temples: the base is a female symbol, and within it stands the phallus. This symbol is rather like the phallic baskets and chests of the Greeks. *The chest or casket is a female symbol, i.e., the womb, a common enough conception in the older mythologies. The chest, barrel, or basket with its precious contents was often thought of as floating on the water, thus forming an analogy to the course of the sun.* The sun sails over the sea like an immortal god who every evening is immersed in the maternal waters and is born anew in the morning... All these sea-going gods are solar figures. They are enclosed in a chest or ark for the "night sea journey (Frobenius), often in the company of a woman – an inversion of the actual situation, but linking up with the theme of continuous cohabitation we met above. During the night sea journey the sun-god is shut up in the mother's womb, and often threatened by all kinds of dangers. (Italics mine, R.B.)[22]

Several points here are of great interest. Firstly, despite Jung's usually maintained conscious identification of the sun with the masculine principle (in phrases like: "The sun sailed over the sea like an immortal god", and: "All these sea-going gods are solar figures"), in the second sentence I have italicised in this last quotation there is a clear 'confession' on his own account of a symbolic identification between the sun floating upon the water and the womb-like, containing images of chest, barrel, basket, ark, etc. The image is ambivalent since, if the sea is a maternal symbol, then the sun or cask which it holds – as it were, 'in its arms' – could be either a masculine 'lover', or a masculine or feminine 'child'. On the other hand, the cask, chest or basket is itself feminine in its function as container, an attribute which can be transferred to the sun too when it is seen on or over the sea, as in many of Thomas's poems and several of Richards's drawings, already discussed. This idea is borne out by numerous traditional mythological images of the sun as a vehicle, whether as boat, ship or chariot: i.e. as a container. Secondly, in the same chapter, Jung also points out that traditional images of paradise and perfection (garden, orchard, holy city, City of the Sun, etc.), which are usually square or circular, and thus also womb-like containers, are also feminine:

> The city is a maternal symbol, a woman who harbours the inhabitants in herself like children... The Old Testament treats the cities of Jerusalem, Babylon, etc., just as if they were women... Strong, unconquered cities are virgins; colonies are sons and daughters. Cities are also harlots.[23]

And so, in *Revelations*, John sees "the holy city, new Jerusalem, coming down from God out of heaven, *prepared as a bride adorned for her husband*". (Italics mine, R.B.)[24] This heavenly bride could well be the sun. In Thomas's poem entitled 'Now', this connection is made explicitly in the equally powerful image of "*the mystic sun, the wife of light,* / The sun that leaps on petals through a nought". (Italics mine, R.B.)[25]

All this bears out our contention that the celestial sun itself, particularly when seen across the sea, is capable of interpretation not only as the god or hero who makes life's journey and is born again, but as the paradisal symbol of the ouranic mother goddess herself, the Queen of Heaven, who is the source and goal of that journey. And apart from the cultural prejudices imposed on our patterns of thinking by received images and associations, we have no cause whatever to assume that the sun in its role of traveller through both heavens and underworld should necessarily be masculine.

Moreover, just as the bowl-shaped *yoni* in Indian temples contains the bole- or pillar-shaped *lingam*,[26] the *Black Apple of Gower* is interpretable as a feminine symbol *containing* the 'seeds' of the masculine. Here, Jung's idea of "continuous cohabitation" links with a fine aperçu by the art critic Robert Melville about Richards's *The Female Contains All Qualities* (fig. 43):

> ...although I would not attempt an explanation of the three forms on the left of the canvas, it occurs to me that it would be profoundly appropriate to the occasion if the larger of the circular forms were *a mandala of successful impregnation*. (Italics mine, R.B.)[27]

If the Black Apple mandala is also a 'womb', could the forms inside it not also indicate the process of mitosis that occurs after fertilisation as soon as the haploid sperm and ovum have fused to form the diploid zygote? Once again, this is genesis: birth and rebirth, and Thomas's "constant building up and breaking down of the images that come out of the central seed, which is in itself destructive and constructive at the same time". Seen in this way, Richards's *Afal du Brogŵyr* is as tantric as any Tibetan or Indian mandala. As Alan Watts says of the sexual act of creation:

> ...in an embrace of this kind, all considerations of time and place, of what and who, drop away, and ... the pair discover themselves as the primordial "love that makes the world go round". There is an extraordinary melting sensation in which "each is both", and, seeing their eyes reflected in each other's they realise that there is one Self looking out through both – *and through all eyes everywhen and everywhere. The conceptual boundary between male and female, self and other, dissolves, and... this particular embrace on this particular day discloses itself as going on forever, behind the scenes.*
> *At the genital centre of the embrace, phallus and vulva form the nucleus of a double helix, which is the pattern of our galaxy.* The two organs seem to change and change about in their roles so that phallus becomes vulva, and vulva becomes phallus. (Italics mine, R.B.)[28]

5   APPLE AND SUN, PARADISE AND ORCHARD

In this respect it is also worth examining in more detail the traditional symbolic connections between the sun and the apple, since both are associated with immortality, resurrection and paradise, and the apple often stands for the sun, growing on the tree in the centre of the archetypal paradisal garden or orchard. Yeats's early poem 'The Song of Wandering Aengus' explores this connection with great delicacy: the speaker in the poem picks a hazel wand in a wood and, with a hazel berry, goes fishing. He catches "a little silver trout" (the same treasure to be found in the waters of the unconscious which we have met earlier). Once it has been landed, the fish turns into a magical maiden:

> ...It had become a glimmering girl
> With apple blossom in her hair
> Who called me by my name and ran
> And faded through the brightening air.
>
> Though I am old with wandering
> Through hollow lands and hilly lands
> I will find out where she has gone,
> And kiss her lips and take her hands;
> And walk among long dappled grass,
> And pluck till time and times are done
> The silver apples of the moon,
> The golden apples of the sun.[29]

Just as in the *Afal du Brogŵyr*, sun and moon here are brought together in the image of the apple: the "glimmering girl" is an immortal love-goddess; fulfilment with her is seen as the goal of life's journey; and among her attributes are "apple blossom". Furthermore, the plucking of the apples of sun and moon implies blissful union with her in paradise. Here Yeats is relying on traditional associations which are extremely old and widespread: golden apples grow in the garden of the Hesperides, and the fruit picked by Eve is an apple in the Judaic Eden myth.

The biblical paradise myth was also important to Thomas, as we have already seen from 'In my genesis' and in the line about "Adam and maiden" quoted from 'Fern Hill'. References to the myth abound in his work. In 'Ceremony After a Fire Raid', for example, he writes: "I know the legend / Of Adam and Eve is never for a second / Silent in my service", and a few lines later, he explicitly makes a connection which offers further reinforcement to our interpretation of the *Afal du Brogŵyr*, by referring to the apple of Eden as "the fruit like a sun".[30] In this 'legend', the apple is clearly associated with the sexual act and the 'knowledge of good and evil' (i.e., understanding of the mysteries of transformation) which sexual awareness both symbolises and brings with it. More specifically, the apple suggests the power of female sexuality, since it is the (wicked) Eve who, tempted by the phallic serpent Satan, first rebels against the patriarch Yahweh by eating the fruit, and so both corrupts and simultaneously initiates her lawfully-wedded husband by passing on to him her illicit knowledge. Thus the eating of the apple symbolises the bliss of sexual awakening and fulfilment for both Adam and Eve. But Eve eats first, so there is a direct suggestion that this fulfilment is specifically – or, at least, originally – that of the female and, what is more, of the female out of monogamous wedlock. But under the rules of a society in which the magical act of naming, as well as property, possessions and privileges, passes from father (Yahweh) to son (Adam), female sexual bliss and abandonment are taboo (or, at least, not mentioned), and must be rigidly clamped within the straitjackets and chastity belts of marriage. In this way, women become, on the one hand, the passive, obedient, receptive carriers both of the male seed and the masculine word, name, law and Logos; and on the other, mysterious and dangerous beings to men, whether daimonic or angelic. In *The Paradise Papers*, subtitled *The Suppression of Women's Rites*, Merlin Stone articulates similar points:

> We are told that, by eating the fruit first, woman possessed sexual consciousness before man and in turn tempted man to partake of the forbidden fruit, that is to join her sinfully in sexual pleasures. This image of Eve as the sexually tempting, but God-defying seductress *was surely induced as a warning to all Hebrew men to stay away from the sacred women of the temples*, for if they succumbed to the temptations of these women, they simultaneously accepted the female deity – Her fruit, her sexuality and, perhaps most important, the resulting matrilineal identity for any children who might be conceived in this manner...
>
> The Hebrew creation myth, which blamed the female of the species for initial sexual consciousness *in order to suppress the worship of the Queen of Heaven, Her sacred women and matrilineal customs*, from that time on assigned to women the role of sexual temptress. It cast her as the cunning and contriving arouser of the physical desires of men, she who offers the appealing but dangerous fruit. In the male religions, sexual drive was not to be regarded as the natural biological desires of men and women that encouraged the species to reproduce itself, but was to be viewed as woman's fault. (Italics mine, R.B.)[31]

Stone's attribution of the taboo on eating the apple, with all its sexual connotations, to repression of the worship of the Queen of Heaven is profoundly revealing. All the same, it must be added that the sweetness of the apple itself survives even in patriarchal myths as a symbol of the unleashing of female sexuality and, by implication, of the generous fecundity of the Earth Mother, which cannot be repressed, even if the Queen of Heaven is replaced by a King for more than a couple of thousand years. And even within Christian tradition, although the woman, Eve, has been made to suffer for her action and experience guilt, shame, pain in childbearing, and so on, she is nonetheless *the agent of the transformation* in Adam – in his 'fortunate fall'. By the very fact of opening his eyes to her own sexual mysteries, it is she who leads him through the "groin of the natural doorway" which opens both in and out of Eden, to orgasm, generation, the world, children, history and death, and ultimately directs him towards the paradisal New Jerusalem, the City of the Sun which is Eden writ large, the earthly garden or orchard transformed into the "heavenly bride adorned for her husband" of John's *Revelations*.

It is of course true that none of this helps the Mother of Humanity, Eve herself, very much in her own human need for fulfilment through sexuality within the patriarchal scheme of things, since her husband remains a jealous one who demands her absolute fidelity, even if in Christian myth (at least in the Orthodox and Catholic churches if not in the Protestant ones) the Daughter of Eve, Mary, herself assumes the role of "heavenly bride" and so is entitled to sit enthroned as Queen of Heaven again alongside her Divine Son Jesus and His Celestial Father, despite her earthly marriage to the mere mortal male, Joseph (her 'infidelity' to him being a neat reversal of Eve's with Satan). The point is that she is only allowed back in heaven on sufferance, whether as the meek and obedient consort and mother to the more important masculine deities, or because she is still a virgin and therefore 'unspotted by sin'; whereas, in previous times, her ancestress the Mother Goddess had reigned there in her own right. Whichever version one prefers, it comes to the same thing: her true femaleness (i.e. her sexuality) has been denied by being sublimated entirely onto a spiritual plane.

This discussion is relevant to Richards and Thomas in a number of ways, the most important in this context being that in the Welsh Nonconformist faith in which they both grew up, there is no feminine presence at all within the celestial panoply to counterbalance Father, Son and Holy Ghost. The Protestant canon provides for no more than the Trinity, consisting of two masculine entities and one neuter one. Within Protestantism, then, the feminine principle is not even sublimated, but repressed entirely. But it does not simply and conveniently disappear because it has been repressed: it merely goes 'underground'; and the more it is repressed, the deeper underground it goes. However, the poets and artists of any society are never merely mouthpieces for an official orthodoxy, as priests and lawyers tend to be; for even when they consciously affirm the existing order, through their symbols they inevitably draw on buried material and give expression to it, thereby "compensating for the cultural canon", as we have seen. This certainly accounts in part for the explosiveness of Richards's 'black sun' in the *Afal du Brogŵyr*. Just as Persephone, the daughter of the Greek Earth Mother, Demeter, goes underground each Winter into the captivating darkness of Hades but is born again each Springtime among the young plants and animals, so through the productions of poets and artists the Queen of Heaven continues secretly to be worshipped even through several thousand 'winters' of patriarchy. And when she re-emerges, she has undergone subtle changes. Her identity is the same, but she is charged with new energy, as in the *Afal du Brogŵyr*. Perhaps this also accounts in part for the constant preoccupation with images of femininity in both Thomas's and Richards's work; and suggests too why many of their symbols are derived from pre-Christian Celtic sources. The *Afal du Brogŵyr* could not have been painted by a Catholic, any more than the *Mona Lisa* by a Protestant. Richards never painted a Madonna, and for all the metaphysical qualities in his finest works and his sensual appreciation of the female form, he never combined these in explicitly Christian images, unless these were overlays or accretions of pre-Christian themes, as in the *Cathédrale Engloutie* series. Richards's best paintings have an eruptive, pagan quality; and for all his references to the Eden myth, so do Thomas's poems.

Sun and apple are closely related, then, and this discussion of their traditional associations reinforces our interpretation of the sun itself as a feminine symbol. We are reminded, perhaps, of Samuel Palmer's painting *The Magic Apple Tree*[32] which, like Yeats's poem, gathers all these associations together: the mysterious golden fruits which cluster in miraculous profusion from its boughs are both a sexual invitation and at the same time hold promise of spiritual transformation to the eater. And the apples in this painting remind one, in turn, of the many breasts of the 2nd century A.D. Roman sculpture of *Diana of Ephesus*,[33] the all-nourishing and all-devouring Earth Mother, with her lower garments and sleeves laden with animals (some of them suggesting the signs of the zodiac, an indication that she has celestial attributes too), and her hands outstretched in a gesture of both bestowing and receiving. In Blake's painting, *Glad Day*, a male human form is framed within a radiant sun, from which he too might be said to be emerging as a 'child from the heavenly womb'.[34] The contemporary Mexican poet, Octavio Paz, also celebrates the transformative power of female sexuality in a cyclical poem which is entitled 'Sunstone';[35] and among Thomas's own sun-images are many which make this connection. Apart from "the meat-eating sun" in 'Twenty Four Years' and "the mystic sun, the wife of light" in 'Now',[36] the 'dark sun' is also identified symbolically with a woman's sexual experience in 'On the Marriage of a Virgin', both in the line: And this day's sun leapt up the sky out of her thighs" and in: "For a man sleeps where fire leapt down and she learns through her arm / That other sun, the jealous coursing of the unrivalled blood".[37]

However, Markale's analysis of the specifically Celtic myths of the Isle of Avalon and of Tristan and Iseult provides the most convincing support for our interpretation of the paradisal and erotic associations of apple and sun in the *Afal du Brogŵyr*. Avalon, or the 'Isle of Apples', was the place King Arthur was taken to after being mortally wounded at the battle of Camlann. Among other sources, Markale quotes Geoffrey of Monmouth's *Vita Merlini*:

> The Isle of Apples was also called Fortunate Isle, because all the vegetation there grew naturally with no need of cultivation... the harvests were rich and the forests thick with apples and grapes... nine sisters ruled over it... and one of them surpassed all the others in beauty and power. Her name was Morgan and she taught how plants could be used to cure illness... Morgan received us with all suitable honours and had the king carried into her room and onto a golden couch... She watched over him a long time, and at last said he would regain his health through her, if he stayed on the island and accepted her cures.[38]

This too is a paradise vision, once again containing the associated motifs of apple trees, fertile vegetation, healing (i.e., both spiritual and physical regeneration), sun (gold) and immortality, all epitomised and brought together in the mysterious and goddess-like figure of Morgan. Avalon is also pictured by Guillaume de Rennes, in the *Gesta Regum Britanniae*, as an island in the ocean – just like Ys, which Richards explored in his *La Cathédrale Engloutie* series. Markale comments:

The island in the ocean, which has all the outward appearances of paradise, is a straightforward symbol, projected into space and removed from the vaguely remembered past to a timeless future, of life inside the womb. Death, illness and old age are unknown. Fruits, particularly apples, grow naturally and abundantly there. In fact, this is the Golden Age that has haunted man's imagination for millenia, the calm and peaceful condition of the foetus protected by the warmth of the mother and fed by her in a secluded world, whether orchard, cave, impregnable fortress or island, where there is as yet no moral life, no distinction between good and evil, no conscious psychic life, and no distinction between self and non-self.

...The remarkable thing about the Celtic paradise was that it remained outside the sphere of influence of the patriarchal structure that, with just a few exceptions, shaped Celtic society. The Isle of Avalon, or its Gaelic equivalent Emain Ablach, was ruled by women in matriarchal organisations. Whether this is a relic of an earlier epoch, either Celtic or pre-Celtic, when woman ruled society, or whether it is the projection of an unconscious desire for *regressus ad uterum* remains an unanswerable question. It is probably both together.[39]

However simplistic the conclusion of this analysis may seem in its orthodox Freudian identification of paradise with a literal 'return to the womb', its tenor certainly fits the *Afal du Brogŵyr* in a lucid and convincing way, and also demonstrates how deeply Richards's consciousness was influenced by his own Celtic origins. Markale nowhere refers to Richards's works, but the parellels between the material he quotes, his analyses, and Richards's recurrent visual motifs, are so consistent that the aptness of his remarks seems much too profound to be merely accidental. The Gower Peninsula itself which surround the 'black apple' could even be interpreted as a partially developed version of the paradisal island of Ys or Avalon. Markale also analyses the Ys legend in depth, once again without referring at all to Richards's work, but in a way that is equally illuminative for an understanding of his *La Cathédrale Engloutie* series. That Richards knew of these Celtic myths which surfaced so forcefully in his work is confirmed by Mrs. Patterson:

As a young child, I was taken to Dunwich (Suffolk) for holidays where there was also a drowned church whose bells were supposed to be heard ringing beneath the waves, so my father was aware of this legend long before he did the *Cathédrale Engloutie* series.

Markale's analysis of the Tristan and Iseult story is even more convincing and once again bears out our interpretation:

> When Tristan wants to meet Iseult without anyone's noticing, he alerts her by throwing shavings of wood into a stream. She then leaves the chamber of her husband, King Mark, and comes to an enclosed orchard where her lover is waiting for her. There, outside the world, Iseult is the sole, omnipotent queen, her hair shining like the rays of the sun in a friendly darkness.
>
> There are further instances of this kind, all apparently happening in a place outside the earth where reigns a queen whose characteristics are *beauty*, *light* and *authority*. The mistress, knowingly tyrannical, always obeyed, never rejected, has at her feet the lover, who "is re-created in the rays from her eyes".
>
> It is important to note the solar nature of the Mistress of the Orchard, whoever she is. Obviously ideas have changed since Max Müller's school of thought made it right and proper to find sun heroes everywhere and to regard mythology as a game of hide and seek with the planets, which in any case explained nothing. But that does not prevent the sun's being inseparable from the Mistress of the Orchard.
>
> First of all, Iseult appears with hair as fair as gold, or as the sun; Grainne's name comes from the Irish *grein*, which means 'sun'. The Queen of the Isle of Fairies lives in a crystal palace, or has a crystal chamber or chamber of glass in which all the rays of the sun converge. When landing on the island, there is a striking impression of light, which seems to rise from the very landscape. So the orchard, which lies in the isle of apple-trees, must be a kind of temple to the sun, where the sun itself lives.
>
> In the Celtic and Germanic languages, the word for sun is feminine, which suggests a female solar divinity whose image has thus survived the creation of the sun god Apollo. Japanese mythology also has a sun goddess, and the ancient divinity of the Scythians was Diana, who was equated with the sun and became the Artemis of the Greeks. Classical writers stressed the bloody and cruel aspects of her worship.
>
> The fate of the sun goddess was inextricably bound up with the rebellion of man against woman, which led to power being vested in a male-dominated, rather than a gynaecocratic, society. There was a total reversal of religious values, the originally feminine divinities being replaced by masculine divinities adapted to the new social structures, of whom the paradigm is Apollo.
>
> There is a strong possibility that the Celts, like the other Indo-Europeans, recognised a sun goddess, who was in fact represented in iconography and inscriptions as the goddess Sul, honoured in Bath (Aquae Sulis). There still remain visible traces of the mother goddess in the various myths in which women take the chief parts – for example, the

story of Tristan and Iseult, and its archetypes and equivalents. So, Iseult, like Grainne and Deirdre, could well be the new and most recent face of the ancient sun goddess, whose image has been perpetuated within a totally male-orientated society.[40]

This is a masterly synthesis, which needs no further comment whatever. But to return to the Judaic tradition, behind the prime-mother of humanity, Eve, there also exists an even older, more shadowy female figure, Lilith, who was the first wife of Adam and was created at the same time as him, but being "dissatisfied because her expectations were not fulfilled", she deserted her spouse and was given to Satan as a wife. Once again, Markale's analysis of this myth throws more light on Richards's apple-symbolism:

> ...Lilith does not disappear completely, but is only driven back into the subconscious to rise again into the conscious mind at the slightest opportunity. And "when Lilith appears again and leaves the shadows of rejection, patriarchal law is confounded. So, when Eve prepared to turn Adam from the true path, it is really Lilith reappearing, and, being the mother of Adam, she feeds him and, occasionally, in tender and erotic mood, plays with his child's penis." (Braunschweig-Fain, *Éros et Antéros*, p.107). The suggestion that Lilith is Adam's mother may seem extravagant, but he must have had a mother to be a human being. Even if he never knew a physical mother he had to create his own image of her; and her flight from him can surely be interpreted as weaning him. The disturbing idea that Lilith was both wife and mother to Adam may explain why she has disappeared from the authorised versions of the Bible. In any case, there is a definite equation between wife and mother. "*The idea of prohibition had been transferred from the game with the genitals to sucking the breast (eating the apple)... The real meaning is 'one may eat the apple but it is forbidden for a son to play sexual games with his mother...'* Who then is Lilith? For Adam she is a first object of love, whom he must not remember, who revealed his sex to him..." (Ibid. pp.107-8.) (Italics mine, R.B.)[41]

Although we may question some of the emphases in Markale's quotation from Braunschweig-Fain, and particularly his insistence on treating the oedipal conflict as primary, the whole of this passage tallies well with Stone's argument that the official version of the Eden myth which has come down to us represents a repression of the worship of feminine deities. More important for us, it offers further hints towards an understanding of why the *Black Apple of Gower* should appear so dark, potent and alarming, and why Jung's language in describing the water-colour is so charged. It is not, merely, that mother-son incest is taboo, for the taboo itself has a history. The reason is that in a patriarchal society like our own, the free expression of female love – and with it, its transformative, creative power on spiritual as well as physical levels – is regarded as a grave threat to the established order or things, and so has to be forced by all the prevailing social and mental pressures that can be mustered into the darkness of the subconscious whenever it threatens to raise its head into the light. And in the repressed zone it assumes nightmarish, destructive and devouring forms to both men and women alike. (In this connection, Mrs. Patterson has told me that Mrs. Frost, who was going to buy the oil-painting as well as the water-colour, decided not to do so as she found the painting "too menacing and frightening".) This point takes us on to one other apparently minor image which is present in all three of the *Afal du Brogŵyr* works and later became dominant for Richards, always relating in some way to Dylan Thomas. This is the owl, which, as we shall see, has profound symbolic resonances, particularly in Celtic tradition, which link in a fully coherent way with all the themes so far explored.

6 OWLS AND OWL MAIDENS

In both the large *Afal du Brogŵyr* oil-painting and the drawing for 'I dreamed my genesis', if one looks carefully, the figure of an owl can be seen lurking embedded in the soil of the Gower Peninsula just to the left of the 'round thing'. It holds a dead, drooping creature between its talons, which in both cases looks like a rabbit or hare, with a head that is decidedly 'phallic' in shape. In the drawing, the owl's talons hold the rabbit around its middle, just as a similar owl holds a dead mouse in the 1953 monoprint for the Sunday Times *Dylan Thomas Memorial Reading* at the Globe Theatre (fig. 24), which must have been made shortly after the *DPDT* drawings. In the large oil-painting, the owl holds the rabbit by its head, but lower down small coiled lines hinting at the form of a human penis also suggest that the rabbit has masculine anthropomorphic connotations, while in the drawing the creature's legs might also be hinting at the human figure. In the 1955 oil-painting *Do not go gentle into that good night* (fig. 25), the dead creature has become explicitly human: a fierce looking owl holds a sheet or shroud in its beak, in which is the broken, buckled body of a dead man; while in the 1965 black and white lithograph of the same title (fig. 27), an owl flies through the night beneath a full or nearly full moon, and below it a naked man falls, head first, into or towards an equally jet black earth or underworld, his hands gesturing horror, his eyes shut tight and his mouth in the shape of a silent scream. These two works are among the most haunting and frightening of Richards's whole artistic career, and both have their origins in the *Afar du Brogŵyr* series. Interestingly, in the water-colour given to Jung (fig. 36), an owl's head and eyes are also suggested at the top of the painting, just to the left of centre above the 'round thing', by the notches in the grain of wood. Such figures also occur in the work of Max Ernst, whom Richards admired and by whom he was influenced.[42] So the petals of the flower that Jung recognised around the central shape could therefore also suggest the shadowy shape of an owl's wings. In the drawing for 'I dreamed my genesis', finny or scaly diagonal lines behind the rabbit's head also suggest the form of a fish, reminding us once more of the heron with the fish in its mouth; and in a 1955 black and white lithograph entitled *Homage to Dylan Thomas* (fig. 25), the night-fishing heron holding an upturned skull with flowers growing out of it in the foreground is haloed by a moon while, above the skull, an owl flies through the sky, holding scraps of paper with lines of poetry written on them.

The associations in this series are as ambiguous and complex as any of the other symbols we have yet encountered in Richards's work; and, as in all other cases, there is no single, casual line of thought that we can follow single-mindedly in order to trace either the provenance or development of the owl-symbolism. The motif could have been sparked off in Richards's mind by Ernst, by his looking closely at the marks of the wood-grain rubbed into the paper on which he was painting, by an image or images in Thomas's poetry, or by all of these. In the 'Author's Prologue', for example, these lines occur:

> Hoo, there, in castle keep,
> You king singsong owls, who moonbeam
> The flickering runs and dive
> The dingle furred dead![43]

Mrs. Patterson has also told me an interesting personal reminiscence that throws more light on the owl in her *Afal du Brogŵyr* oil-painting:

I remember when I was a child, I was with my father once when we saw an owl suddenly flying out of one of those caves down on the Gower coast. It was quite a thrill, and it's still very clear in my memory. I think it must have excited my father too. I think the owl in the painting is holding a rabbit, because the hills along that coastline used to be full of rabbits... I also think that one of the other reasons he picked on that particular symbol (like the heron) in the poems, was that he loved them as birds.

All these pieces of information help build up a picture of Richards's feeling for owls, and how and where he encountered them, but they indicate neither why they became so important to him that he produced at least half a dozen works containing the owl as a motif, nor why these were always associated with Dylan Thomas, nor why the responses they generate in us as viewers should be so eerie. Once again, what understanding is possible must be built up syncretistically and in relationship to the other symbols that occur with and around the owl, both in Richards's own work and in that of others.

Like the heron, this bird of night is also a hunter, a predator, and in this respect some of the symbolism attached to the owl must also connect with themes we have explored already, particularly as far as the phallic and 'fish-like' elements of its prey are concerned. But in its emotional impact on us, the owl is far more frightening than the graceful heron: shunned or attacked by day-birds, it is linked with the loneliness and darkness of death, and Richards makes full use of these associations. Furthermore, it is a killer not primarily of aquatic creatures, but of warm-blooded land-mammals and, therefore, by implication – at least on a symbolic level – of humans, inspiring us with fear and awe. And since the owl's prey in Richards's paintings and drawings is usually masculine, whether explicitly or by more delicate suggestion, in terms of polarities it is likely that its own symbolism in his work should be predominantly feminine: an interpretation that is borne out both by its round head and body, and also by the way in which Richards offsets it in some designs with the presence of the 'phallic', 'masculine' heron.

These remarks also find support in Erich Neumann's study of the feminine archetype, *The Great Mother*, where he suggests that the owl's traditionally feminine symbolism is at least in part related to the "uterine form" of its body. He also notes that "it is impossible for us to decide whether the night owl is a feminine symbol of the night sky or whether it is the moon itself".[44] and says of the Great Goddess that "for milleniums she stands or sits enthroned upon lions, as the Mesopotamian goddess Lilith of night, evil and death, winged, bird-footed, and accompanied by owls".[45] Just as the golden lion is a symbol of the Sun-God, so the owl is an emblem of the Goddess of Death herself: the bird who kills in the darkness of night, beneath the moon, and carries off her prey through the air. But in her latter aspect, symbolically she is not only death but also the winged carrier of souls to the underworld, where, like the sun, they travel slowly back to dawn and rebirth. Cirlot reinforces this interpretation, with a comment that is still more astonishingly apt in relation to the 'black sun' motif in the *Afal du Brogŵyr*:

> In the Egyptian system of hieroglyphs, the owl symbolised death, night, cold and passivity. *It also pertains to the realm of the dead sun, that is, of the sun which has set below the horizon and which is crossing the lake or sea of darkness.* (Italics mine, R.B.)[46]

However, to return to specifically Celtic motifs, there is an even richer vein of associations to explore in owl-symbolism. For, as in the water-colour given to Jung, owls and flowers are closely linked in the myth of Blodeuwedd, the maiden made from flowers who is turned into an owl in the same Welsh story of 'Math Son of Mathonwy' in *The Mabinogion* which we have already discussed in connection with Thomas's namesake Dylan Eil Ton. This theme, incidentally, has been richly mined by Alan Garner in his fine novel for teenagers, also set in his native Wales, entitled *The Owl Service*,[47] and it is sad that Richards did not live to illustrate it: he would have done so superbly. The myth is similar to that of Tristan and Iseult and of Lilith/Eve and Satan, in that it concerns marital infidelity on the part of a woman in a society which has recently shifted to a patriarchal system. The background to the story is neatly summarised by Markale:

> Arianrod, daughter of Don, gave birth to two sons, Dylan and Lleu, whom she refused to recognise. Dylan threw himself into the sea and drowned, while Lleu was brought up by his uncle, Gwyddyon, Arianrod's brother and probably also her lover. She had pronounced a curse on her son to the effect that he would have no woman of the race of men. So, with the help of his uncle, the magician Math, Gwyddyon tried to find a way of overcoming the taboo imposed by Arianrod. "They gathered the flowers of the oak tree, of broom and of meadowsweet, which they used, with their spells, to fashion the most perfect maiden in the world", whom they married to Lleu Llaw Gyffes.[48]

Unfortunately, things began to go wrong when Blodeuwedd, the flower-maiden, fell in love with another man, Gronw, Lord of Penlynn in Merioneth, and slept with him and refused to let him go. The lovers then plotted to kill Blodeuwedd's husband Lleu; but when Gronw struck him dead with his javelin, Lleu flew off in the shape of a bird. Gwyddyon managed to find the bird, an eagle – which, like the lion, is also a golden 'masculine' sun symbol, and clearly the symbolic opposite of the 'feminine' owl of darkness. He realised that the eagle was really Lleu, and magically turned him back into human form. Finally he caught up with the guilty lovers, and Gronw with all his retinue was drowned in a river: a neat revenge, perhaps, for the drowning of Dylan Eil Ton, Lleu's brother. As for Blodeuwedd, her fate is described as follows:

> And then Gwydion overtook her too, and he said to her: "I will not slay thee. I will do to thee that which is worse; that is" said he, "I will let thee go in the form of a bird. And because of the dishonour thou hast done to Lleu Llaw Gyffes thou art never to dare show thy face in the light of day, and that through fear of all birds; and that there be an enmity between thee and all birds, and that it be their nature to mob and molest thee wherever they may find thee; and that thou shalt not lose thy name, but that thou be for ever called Blodeuwedd."
>
> Blodeuwedd is 'owl' in the language of this present day. And for that reason birds are hostile to the owl. And the owl is still called Blodeuwedd.[49]

And as the translators point out, Blodeuwedd means "Flower-face, no bad name for the owl".

Markale's complex and masterly analysis of this myth is too long to give a detailed account of here.[50] To summarise, however: the creation of Blodeuwedd by Gwyddyon and Math out of flowers is as *unnatural* as that of Lilith by Yahweh out of clay, Eve from Adam's spare rib or Pandora by Prometheus out of fire stolen from Zeus – or, for that matter, of the divine Athena out of her father Zeus's forehead (two of Athena's attributes also being the serpent and the owl). It seems likely that all these tales articulate the attempts of a relatively newly established and still somewhat shaky patriarchy to assert its dominance over a previously authoritative gynaeocracy by the simple magical device of stealing from women their mysterious (and to men, frightening) child-bearing abilities, and usurping these into the masculine domain, thereby belittling or denying altogether the social importance of women. It seems equally likely that many feminine deities like Athena, Diana-Artemis etc. antedate the Olympian-type mas-culine theogonies in which most of them have come down to us, and that their earlier characteristics have been distorted and limited in the process of assimilation into patriarchal systems. It is also probable that in their earliest form, these patriarchal stories were related to the scientific discovery of the connection between the sexual act and procreation, which meant that patrilineage could be established. But this discovery, apparently, involved the suppression of other, equally important 'facts of life': the role of the womb and all aspects of maternal nurturing.

Thus the creation of daughter figures like Lilith, Eve, Pandora, Athena, Blodeuwedd, etc. in patriarchal myths and theogonies all runs counter to the 'real facts of life' and suggests the taking over of natural and instinctual processes by loftier 'intellectual' or 'spiritual' patterns of behaviour. All these daughters have one thing in common: they are *man-made*, as fully formed young women with their sexual attributes already developed. In this way they could serve as useful commodities for the male characters in the stories, in the bargaining for dowries which accompanied marriages. These daughters *had no childhoods and no mothers*, which is to say that their consciousness of their real origins had been repressed, and they could therefore easily be manipulated as useful and pliant tools or playthings to fit in with the requirements and whims of the patriarchs. They are all, in a sense, the offspring of 'planned families', that is to say, the products of thinking and of industry, of *cunning* and *craft*; and, as such, they are not only "symbolic of the great upheaval that took place in some distant and hazy period of antiquity or prehistory, when the cult of a father god replaced the cult of the mother-goddess, and male-oriented, patriarchal society replaced a female-orientated gynaeocracy",[51] but of periods of early *social, scientific and industrial revolution*. While this interpretation should in no way imply that these complex daughter-figures are 'merely allegorical' representations of such historical processes, the myths do make their points simply and clearly: Pandora was manufactured from fire, just as Lilith was manufactured from clay. This implies cookery, pottery and the use of the kiln for baking and perhaps also smelting. Eve was extracted from Adam's side in the form of a rib, which implies surgery and perhaps also mining. Athena too was extracted from her father's forehead, which also implies surgery. Nor should it be forgotten that the forehead is the zone of the intellect rather than the instincts: the role of the womb has been taken over

93

by that of the brain. Blodeuwedd was made out of flowers, which suggests agriculture and gardening. Even if some of these activities were originally carried out by women in early societies, many were gradually taken over by men.

In the Blodeuwedd story, however, the older female-dominated social order fights back, in the person of Arianrod who, according to Markale, is "one of the faces of the mother goddess",[52] an idea which, interestingly for us, perhaps also throws further light on the character of Dylan Eil Ton, whose mother she was. It would perhaps be tempting to argue, in the neo-Freudian terms adopted by Markale (even though he himself attacks Freud as an 'anti-feminist': see p.95 below), that Ariadrod both vengefully embodies the 'oedipal conflict' which recognition of the fact of fatherhood brings with it, and attempts to reverse the taboo on 'mother-son' incest' which the new male-dominated order imposes. However, such an interpretation fails to take account of other important motifs in the myth,[53] since Ariadrod herself has rejected her own motherhood in favour of a 'magical virginity', which hardly suggests the simple role of the possessive, witch-like mother fighting for her child, which is so appealing to the modern male, even though her virginal and magical attributes could well indicate her devotion and service to a feminine deity. Apart from these objections, the Freudian insistence on taking 'mother-son incest' literally in any story of this kind necessarily involves both distortion and oversimplification, as Jung makes clear:

> The so-called "incest prohibition" which is supposed to operate here is not in itself a primary phenomenon, but *goes back to something much more fundamental, namely the primitive system of marriage classes which, in its turn, is a vital necessity in the organisation of the tribe.* So it is more a question of phenomena requiring a teleological explanation than of simple causalities. *Moreover it must be pointed out that the basis of the "incestuous" desire is not cohabitation, but, as every sun myth shows, the strange idea of becoming a child again, of returning to the parental shelter, and of entering into the mother in order to be reborn through her... It is not incestuous cohabitation that is desired, but rebirth.* (Italics mine, R.B.)[54]

This suggests that the desire for the 'paradisal mother-bride' which we have traced in Thomas's sun-images may well also be rooted in a yearning for a previous, very ancient and long-lost social order, in which the love between mother and child was not repressed. As a further aside here, it is interesting to note how revolutionary the new hope of Christianity must have been, since it promised to accord to women their own valued place in the patriarchal scheme of things through the phenomenon of virgin birth, redeeming them from the stain of Eve by implying that they could all become as blessed as Mary simply by continuing their traditional role as passive carriers of both male seed and masculine property, etc. Mary's impregnation not by her human spouse Joseph but by the spiritual seed of the couple's Celestial Overlord (a neat mythical encapsulation of the *Droit du Seigneur* which thrived in Europe right through the Christian Middle Ages) represents an equal falsification of the real facts, in order to perpetuate the image of an all-powerful, but now apparently, all-beneficent father-god. Perhaps this explains why early Christianity was initially so popular among women – and slaves. The Assumption of the Virgin perhaps represented a policy of appeasement by assimilation towards a potential opposition.[55]

Not surprisingly, Arianrod fails. But her struggle is taken on by Blodeuwedd herself, the daughter of the new clan-system in which the woman is supposed to be the property of the males. For Blodeuwedd has not forgotten her own womanly instincts and feelings, which cannot be denied; and although she too fails in the end and, like Lilith and Eve, is condemned to a life of guilt and shame, she too tries to rebel against the patriarchy by choosing a fulfilled though illicit love rather than a marriage arranged by the fathers. Thus, as Markale puts it:

> ...there is only one solution open to Gwyddyon, to change Blodeuwedd into an owl, a bird of the night, *thereby banishing her into the shadows. To put it more simply, the father expels the rebellious daughter into the shadows of the subconscious...* Just as Blodeuwedd could rise at any time from concealment in Gwyddyon's subconscious to his conscious mind, so the rebellion of the Flower-Daughter poses a constant threat to the foundations of patriarchal society, even if it remains unmentioned or condemned by reality. This is one of the reasons why man is so frightened of woman and why he deliberately leaves her in a state of inferiority and unconsciousness of her powers. *It is better that she never knows she can rebel, nor realises that the myth of Blodeuwedd is the myth of every woman, and that there is indeed a* Blodeuwedd complex *about which the anti-feminist Freud never spoke.* (My italics, R.B.)[56]

The relevance of this analysis to Richards's work could not be more striking: Most of all, it offers helpful insights into the symbolic relationship between the owl and the 'round thing' in the *Afal du Brogŵyr* series, for here the owl is still embedded in the darkness of the earth, still "banished into the shadows of the subconscious", still waiting for release from its under-ground cave, in precisely the same zone of repression and taboo from which the 'womb' of the 'black apple' is still struggling to free itself and rise to the surface of consciousness again, through several thousand years of masculine dominated myths and culture. But not only this: as we have suggested, in Jung's water-colour, the hint of an owl's head and wings lurks *in the grain and notches of the wood-pattern itself*, among the shadows behind the petals of the flower that surround the 'round thing'. As Jung says in his letter to Richards, "The background (wood) points to matter", i.e., to the earth in which flowers grow; and so, just as in the Blodeuwedd myth, this owl too is connected with the abundant images of sun-like flowers which spread as agents of metamorphosis through the pages of *DPDT* and into all of Richards's later work throughout the 'sixties and until his death: in the *Cathédrale Engloutie* series, in his lithographs and paintings based on poems by Vernon Watkins, especially the visionary 'Music of Colours, White Blossom',[57] and into all the works with titles like *Blossom, Green Metaphor, Origin of Species* (fig. 46), and so on.

As for the owl herself in Richards's later work, she flies free into the night and, gradually, is reunited with her masculine counterpart, the heron who plucks flowers out of the sea in an upturned skull and so transforms death into life again. We have already shown the symbolic identification between the poet's words and flowers, and when the owl bears in her beak scraps of paper on which are written lines of poems, as in the 1955 lithograph (fig. 25), it may be argued that, symbolically, *the owl too bears flowers again* and so also becomes a transformative agent, replacing the bush festooned with scraps of poetry in the 1954 drawing (fig. 23). Although she steals both poet and his poems away in the dead of night, she will scatter his words on the wind like seeds or blossoms. Thus, as an agent of death, the owl is not wholly negative in character in Richards's work, eerie though she may be: death implies rebirth, which flowers always symbolise. Through the Blodeuwedd myth, we therefore see that Richards's concern, like Alan Garner's in *The Owl Service*, is to redeem the Owl-Maiden from darkness, to fill the rooms of our minds as fragrantly as that of Garner's young heroine, Alison's, is filled: "full of petals from skylight and rafters, and all about them a fragrance, and petals, flowers falling, broom, meadowsweet, falling, flowers of the oak".[58] Thus the owl, devourer of mammals, and the face of the mother goddess in one of her most savage forms, becomes the bearer and planter of seeds of dawn and wisdom. To put this another way, the *cultural* transformation that Richards's paintings and drawings celebrate is nothing less than the full liberation and flowering of the repressed feminine side of contemporary consciousness, in both females and males, through its own "struggle from darkness towards some measure of light" which the twenty year-old Thomas saw as his poet's role, and which the *Black Apple of Gower* epitomises.

7   THE APPLE AND IMAGES OF FEMININITY

We have now come nearly to the end of this investigation, but, before we arrive, there is also conclusive internal evidence from Richards's own artistic development to support our argument that the central impetus in the *Afal du Brogŵyr* series, and, in fact, in all his work taken as a coherent corpus, is celebration of female sexuality and exploration of this as a metaphor for the liberation of qualities of behaviour in our society which are traditionally regarded as feminine. A similar point is made, though with a different emphasis, by Robert Melville:

> The image of a ravished female figure, which becomes explicit in the *Rape of the Sabines* series is, I believe, the image from which all his curvilinear forms derive their behaviour. She is, in a sense, the 'sacred prostitute' of his art, lending herself to all the forms that pass through his imagination, even to those splayed-out water-patterns ... in the *Cathédrale Engloutie* paintings: and since she frequently allows herself to be torn to pieces, she is also present in the fragmented water-patterns.
>
> We can perhaps more easily detect her impress upon less explicit forms if we first take a look at the figures in the *Rape of the Sabines* series. No one would expect a modern painter to give the theme a mock-historical treatment, and in Richards's versions it is a rite, with a dithyrambic character, wild and vehement. The male figures are of course subsidiary to the females, who perform flights of yielding heads falling back, breasts waving, limbs flying. They are not simply being carried off, they are being 'carried away', transported in the sense of being enraptured, and in precisely the same sense, ravished.
>
> With these paintings and drawings in mind, it would be very difficult not to recognise the image of a ravished female figure in the marvellous

painting entitled *The Female Contains All Qualities...*

It will be seen, I think, that the imprint of the ravished female figure on Richards's most recent paintings remains as ineradicable as ever, informing all the innocent leaves and blossoms with her rapture; transforming them into marvellous dithyrambs on the Pleasure Principle...[59]

Melville is clearly right in interpreting even the most abstract and non-figurative works of Richards, as well as his motifs of "fragmented water-patterns" and "innocent leaves and blossoms", as feminine symbols; and in this respect his remarks are entirely to the point. I disagree with him, however, in taking the images of the *Rape of the Sabines* as primary, since the theme of 'ravishment', with all its overtones of violence, is by no means the only aspect of relationships between the sexes that Richards treated during his prolific career. To attribute to Richards the image of rape as a model for sexual behaviour is surely to impute a male chauvinist shallowness and sentimentality to him, rather than the more profound searching for "metaphors for the nature of existence" and "for the secrets of our time"[60] which he himself believed he was involved in, and which his works exemplify, including the *Rapes* series. Apart from this, many of his figurative images of girls and women, either alone or with accompanying males, are gentle and compassionate (for example, figs. 1, 2, 13, and most of all the sleeping girl lying amid flowers in fig. 31, who could well represent an image of Blodeuwedd herself). The *Rapes* series were composed between 1947 and 1949, in the years following the Second World War, and their raw, aggressive quality must surely also relate to that. Furthermore, although Melville hints at a symbolic interpretation, he does not carry it through to a consideration of what the symbols might signify in terms of broader historical transformations, since images of femininity are not to be interpreted merely literally, and less still, by any easy reference to a "Pleasure Principle". For, despite the underlying truth in this – that Richards, like Thomas, celebrates the *instincts* in his work, not the intellect divorced from the instincts – the Freudian idea of the "Pleasure Principle" can all too easily serve as a justification for a repressive social and economic order in which prostitutes, whether sacred or not, serve to prop up a corrupt, male-dominated hierarchy whose stated values are all 'high', 'noble', 'spiritual', 'intellectual', and so on, but in fact are based on exploitation, cunning and the mechanistic repression of feeling, instinct and true spirituality, which, in his poem 'London', Blake called "the mind-forg'd manacles", continuing:

But most thro' midnight streets I hear
How the youthful Harlot's curse
Blasts the new born Infant's tear,
And blights with plagues the Marriage hearse.[61]

In fact, there are no "sacred prostitutes" in our society, if there have ever been in any male-dominated social order. Prostitutes are subject to risk and abuse within and without the law.

The internal evidence for Richards's concern with femininity is to be found mainly in the occurrence of the swirling 'fig-like' shapes in both earlier and later work, which also appear within the 'round thing' itself in the *Afal du Brogŵyr* series. In this connection, it is interesting to refer to Merlin Stone again, who suggests that "the tree of knowledge of good and evil in earliest times was not an apple but a fig", and points out that not only did Adam and Eve wear fig-leaves to hide their shame, but that "the fig-tree was regarded as a gift given by the Goddess" in other parts of the ancient world.[62] Whether she is right or not about the Eden myth, her comment is further support for our interpretation of Richards's work. Symbols operate by accretion of associations, and in Richards's 'round thing' both apple and fig are represented.

The fig-like forms are already present in highly abstract and geometrical motifs most of the *Relief Constructions* and *The Sculptor and His Studio* series of the 'thirties. Where the 'object' or model the artist or sculptor contemplates is not figuratively portrayed as a female nude, some combinations of attributes like breasts, nipples, womb, vagina, etc. are always present or hinted at symbolically (as in fig. 45, a work dated 1934). The 1937 oil-painting *The Female Contains All Qualities* (fig. 43) also contains circular forms which are strikingly similar to those inside the 'round thing' in the *Afal du Brogŵyr*, and so does the leafy, burgeoning, alembic-like figure on the left in the 1947 lithograph, *Two Females* (fig. 44). This 'plant-lady' also rests her knee on an apple, split in half to reveal the pips and core, while her topmost leaves or petals contain and protect a semi-figurative female nude, who appears to be just emerging. As we have already noted, the shape of the fig, or of 'heart-within-testicles-within-heart', which is also suggestive of both breasts and vagina, is present too in the three 1945 lithographs for *Poetry London* (figs. 40-42), and particularly in the double-page centre-piece; and these forms also reappear as late as 1971 in the screenprint *Origin of Species* (fig. 46), both in the apple-shaped bulb on the left and in the heart of the figure on the right, which connects by stems to both nipples and womb in a manner almost tantric. The unworked line-drawings for 'I dreamed my genesis' from both the Swansea version and Mrs. Thomas's version of the *Collected Poems* (figs. 37 and 38), in which the 'round thing' is held or caught between the hands like a ball or an enormous seed or nut (reminding one of the lines: "Wild men, who caught and sang the sun in flight / And learn, too late, they grieved it on its way" in 'Do not go gentle into that good night'[63]), confirm these connections beyond doubt. Many more examples could be given but these are enough to make the point that the forms perfected in the *Afal du Brogŵyr* oil-painting recur throughout Richards's career, and are always predominantly feminine in their symbolism.

8   THE APPLE AND TRANSFORMATION :
ENDS AND BEGINNINGS

In his autobiography, Jung describes a period in 1916 when he was 'haunted' by a number of "strange occurrences", which resulted in an extraordinary work entitled *Septem Sermones ad Mortuos* ('Seven Sermons to the Dead').[64] Both he and members of his family had been experiencing unusually vivid fantasies and dreams: a fisherman who had caught a fish; the soul having flown away; and so on. Jung continues with this account:

> Around five o'clock in the afternoon on Sunday the front-door bell began ringing frantically. It was a bright summer day; the two maids were in the kitchen, from which the open square outside the front door could be seen. Everyone immediately looked to see who was there, but there was no-one in sight. I was sitting near the door bell, and not only heard it but saw it moving. We all simply stared at one another. The atmosphere was thick, believe me! Then I knew that something had to happen. The whole house was filled as if there were a crowd present, crammed full of spirits. They were packed deep right up to the door, and the air was so thick it was scarcely possible to breathe. As for myself, I was all a-quiver with the question: "For God's sake, what in the world is this?" Then they cried out in chorus, "We have come back from Jerusalem where we found not what we sought." That is the beginning of the *Septem Sermones*.
>
> Then it began to flow out of me, and in the course of three evenings the thing was written. As soon as I took up the pen, the whole ghostly assemblage evaporated. The room quieted and the atmosphere cleared. The haunting was over.[65]

The importance of the writing of this text for Jung, and of its accompanying fantasies, is hard to underestimate in the light of his comments which follow:

> When I look back on it now and consider what happened to me during the period of my work on the fantasies, it seems as though a message had come to me with overwhelming force. There were things in the images which concerned not only myself but many others also. It was then that I ceased to belong to myself alone, ceased to have the right to do so. From then on, my life belonged to the generality. The knowledge I was concerned with, or was seeking, still could not be found in the science of those days. I myself had to undergo the original experience, and, moreover, try to plant the results of my experience in the soil of reality; otherwise they would have remained subjective assumptions without validity. It was then that I dedicated myself to service of the psyche. I loved it and hated it, but it was my greatest wealth. My delivering myself over to it, as it were, was the only way by which I could endure my existence and live it as fully as possible.
>
> Today I can say that I have never lost touch with my initial experiences. All my works, all my creative activity, has come from those initial fantasies and dreams ... Everything that I accomplished in later life was already contained in them, although at first only in the form of emotions and images.[66]

The text of *Septem Sermones ad Mortuos* itself is a symbolist prose-poem, and represents the only concession Jung ever made to the direct expression of his own poetic genius. It celebrates a god whom "mankind forgot", whose name, 'ABRAXAS', is clearly reminiscent of the magical alphabetical spell 'Abracadabra'. The passage in *Septem Sermones ad Mortuos* about this strange entity, with its imagery of sun, darkness and transformation, is so close to that of the *Afal du Brogŵyr* that it perhaps throws more light on the painting than either his letter to Richards or any of his other more scholarly discussions of symbol-formation and psychic processes. "*It is force, duration, change,*" he writes, and continues:

> *Abraxas is the sun, and at the same time the eternally sucking gorge of the void, the belittling and dismembering devil.*
> The power of Abraxas is twofold; but ye see it not, because for your eyes the warring opposites of this power are extinguished.
>
> What the god-sun speaketh is life.
> What the devil speaketh is death.

But Abraxas speaketh that hallowed and accursed word which is life and death at the same time.

Abraxas begetteth truth and lying, good and evil, light and darkness, in the same word and in the same act. Wherefore is Abraxas terrible.

It is splendid as the lion in the instant he striketh down his victim.
It is beautiful as a day of spring.

It is the great Pan himself and also the small one.
It is Priapos.
It is the monster of the underworld, a thousand armed polyp, coiled knot of winged serpents, frenzy.
It is the hermaphrodite of the earliest beginning.

...It is abundance that seeketh union with emptiness.
It is holy begetting.
It is love and love's murder.
It is the saint and his betrayer.
It is the brightest light of day and the darkest night of madness.

To look upon it, is blindness.
To know it, is sickness.
To worship it, is death.
To fear it, is wisdom.
To resist it not, is redemption.

...It is the son's horror of the mother.
It is the mother's love for the son.
It is the delight of the earth and the cruelty of the heavens.
Before its countenance man becometh like stone.
Before it there is no question and no reply.

It is the life of creatura.
It is the operation of distinctiveness.
It is the love of man.
It is the speech of man.
It is the appearance and the shadow of man.
It is illusory reality.[67]

The lines I have italicised in particular show almost uncanny similarities to the *Afal du Brogŵyr*. Just as in the painting, we have here a composite symbol of great power, and its terrifying aspects, I would suggest, all relate to the same theme we have explored in detail throughout this monograph: the repressed images of femininity, which are dangerous and daimonic in our culture *only* because they are repressed. The god whom "mankind forgot" could well have been a goddess. All of this suggests that the "secret of our time" which Jung believed Richards's painting 'confessed', and which so fascinated and disconcerted him, was none other than the full emancipation of women from their traditional roles in a society dominated by patriarchal attitudes, and of both men and women from stereotyped beliefs in the symbols which underly these roles: a much needed transformation of *mores* and behaviour which we now see taking place in every sphere of our lives, amid great upheaval and often involving suffering. Jung, who was one of the greatest creative minds of this century, was no less its child than any of us, and no less subject to the kind of psychic disturbance expressed in *Septem Sermones and Mortuos* and described analytically years later in his autobiography. Richards, who was equally a child of his time, expressed a very similar psychic upheaval in the *Afal du Brogŵyr*; and Jung's ascription of a 'confession' to Richards's painting is itself his own confession of the power the archetype exerted over him, just as he saw it exerted over his contemporaries. For if, as Jung and Neumann would have it, Richards's work, like that of any great artist, is to be understood best in terms of "conjuring up the forms in which the age is most lacking" and "compensating for the inadequacy and one-sidedness of the present" in order to restore health, then the 'lack', 'inadequacy' and 'one-sidedness' are all on the side of contemporary consciousness, with its over-valuing of intellect at the expense of the 'deeper' zones of the instincts and basic passions, which are just as important keys to the 'higher' spiritual zones as the intellect itself. Our traditionally 'positive' images of intellect and consciousness themselves are usually equated with masculinity, and they stultify and imprison us within our own self-approval, which is all too neatly and tautologously reflected through them. Correspondingly, we are constricted in thought and behaviour by images which embody feminine qualities as 'negative' and identify these with instinct and passion. Both masculine and feminine qualities need to flourish, and to do so within us together and in harmony. As Neumann writes:

> ...This problem of the Feminine has equal importance for the psychologist of culture, who recognizes that the peril of present-day mankind springs in large part from the one-sidedly patriarchal development of the male intellectual consciousness, which is no longer kept in balance by the matriarchal world of the psyche...

Western mankind must arrive at a synthesis that includes the feminine world – which is also one-sided in its isolation. Only then will the individual human being be able to develop the psychic wholeness that is urgently needed if Western man is to face the dangers that threaten his existence from within and without.[68]

Ceri Richards, like Dylan Thomas, did not flinch from this task. And what his work says to us by its example, through all its complex symbolic associations, is really very simple: that it is the job of the artist and poet to lift our jaded images of femininity out of the secret places we have hidden them in, to air them afresh, to rethink and reinterpret them, and to follow them, not blindly, but awarely, and so ourselves become creative, embodying creation and self-transformation in the core and every corner of our lives, and in our ends as in our beginning.

As for ends and beginnings, in May 1980, after I had completed the first draft of this monograph, I met Mrs. Esther Thomas, Ceri Richards's sister. These were her remarks, in conversation, about the *Afal du Brogŵyr* oil-painting:

> I can remember discussing that painting with Ceri, and that little rocky beach with the sand on the beach. I can remember it so well. It reminds me of the Three Cliffs. We talked about it. The sand going in and out of the rocks in the painting is just like the sea in Gower... When an apple drops from the tree, if it's left and not disturbed it becomes quite black, and eventually it will rot and disappear and the seed is left, and here is the beginning of the new plant. I can remember Ceri telling me that. Eventually it disintegrates and it's a seed, and it's already in the soil and then you're left with the next seed – the new apples... Some people find that painting disturbing. I don't find it disturbing. I find it has the essence of life in it – the beginning, the end, and the beginning again – and to me that's how all life happens: the end of the visual and the physical, but there's something going on that's out of sight. I think that. I feel that. Without an end, there's no beginning, and without a beginning, you don't have an end either...

The *Black Apple of Gower*, then, must surely be one of the richest and most powerful symbols in 20th century Western art. It is both the earth's core and a growth within the earth, the cross-section of a fruit, root or stem growing simultaneously into it and higher out of it, as the 'child' or 'lover' of the earth-mother. It is the opening of a cave, well or hole in the earth, the entrance to the underworld which is the realm of both death and rebirth, a vertical avenue leading to the "centre of the earth" and the "beginning of the world" and of all creation in time and space, where all beginnings are ends, all ends beginnings, and all oppositions are cancelled out. It is the chthonic womb which is both source, way and goal: it is not only the cave-mouth but the cave itself, not only the gateway to the underworld but the underworld itself, not only the vagina but the womb itself, in which is contained all the seeds or pips of creation, the "central seed" that is "destructive and constructive at the same time". It is an image of "continuous cohabitation", of the act of physical love, the genital embrace between earth and sky, by moon and sun, of *lingam* and *yoni*, phallus and vulva, sperm and ovum joining, and of the cells of the newly formed embryo dividing and multiplying. It is the little death and the great death, genesis and apocalypse, "the legend of Adam and maiden". And in its death-aspect it is frightening – accompanied by an owl, the wise bird of night who is both devourer of mammals, mistress of death and bearer of the soul of the dead to the underworld; though it is simultaneously a sun-like flower growing out of the underworld, new life, resurrection. It is the flower that blooms by night, the precious jewel buried in the rock and it is the dark, impenetrable rock itself in which the jewel is to be found, which defies the prospector by its hardness and resilience. And it is both the light of a newly emerging consciousness as yet held back by the gravitational pull of the unconscious, the alchemical *prima materia* or nigredo out of which all consciousness emerges and to which it must return, the alembic in which alchemical transmutations take place, and the *lapis philosophorum* itself, the philosophers' stone or magical gold that is the goal of the search – gnosis, knowledge of Self, Σοφία, wisdom – and it is also the terrifying face of the collective unconscious itself, of the deepest, most primitive and invisible instincts underlying all the achievements of consciousness and civilisation. It is the companion and enantiomorph of the celestial sun, the sun at night, black and buried beneath the earth's rim and surrounded by the ocean because at night the celestial sun has died and sails its ship or steers its chariot across the waters of the underworld before the dawn of its new life. And it is both dawn and dusk, sunset and sunrise, the zone in which sun and moon meet, mate and merge. It is transformation, "the creation of creating", on all the levels of manifestation in the cosmos, that zone or point in space-time where all synchronicities occur, when the manifest joins with the unmanifest and being becomes not-being and turns back into being again: the maw-like 'black hole' in which matter meets antimatter, *yang* meets *yin* and masculine meets feminine. And it is the tap-root both of cultural artefacts and achievements like art and poetry, and of the historical transformations in consciousness and behaviour which poetry and art grow from, are nourished by and in turn express and mirror but never exhaust, particularly insofar as these concern gender and the roles played out, through history, by men and women who are conditioned beyond (and beneath) our knowledge by such received symbols. In drawing its strength from ancient myths which relate passion and struggle, between Blodeu-wedd and Gwyddyon, Lilith and Yahweh, it pulls our attention back to the forces and patterns underlying them; yet, at the same time, and even more crucially, it comments on and enacts the passions and struggles of our own era, which it draws its strength from equally, celebrating the possibility of an achievement through them which, though within our grasp, is as yet only envisaged, not yet won: the full integration of femininity into conscious-ness, not as another oppressor, but as the peer and partner of masculinity, in mutual recognition, freedom and respect, through love and through justice. And it is the wheel, our round of nights and days. As we look into it, turning, we see it look back at us. It watches us through its single eerie eye.

Gravesend and Cambridge,
November 1979 – January 1980,
and January – February 1981.

Illustrations

CERI RICHARDS *Drawings to Poems by Dylan Thomas* ENITHARMON

1

Especially when the October wind
(Some let me make you of autumnal spells,
The spider-tongued, and the loud hill of Wales)
With fists of turnips punishes the land,
Some let me make you of the heartless words.
The heart is drained that, spelling in the scurry
Of chemic blood, warned of the coming fury.
By the sea's side hear the dark-vowelled birds.

17

2

In my Craft or Sullen Art

IN my craft or sullen art
Exercised in the still night
When only the moon rages
And the lovers lie abed
With all their griefs in their arms,
I labour by singing light
Not for ambition or bread
Or the strut and trade of charms
On the ivory stages
But for the common wages
Of their most secret heart.

Not for the proud man apart
From the raging moon I write
On these spindrift pages
Nor for the towering dead
With their nightingales and psalms
But for the lovers, their arms
Round the griefs of the ages,
Who pay no praise or wages
Nor heed my craft or art.

128

3

1 Back and front cover design for *DPDT*   2 and 3 designs for *DPDT*

Author's Prologue

This day winding down now
At God speeded summer's end
In the torrent salmon sun,
In my seashaken house
On a breakneck of rocks
Tangled with chirrup and fruit,
Froth, flute, fin and quill
At a wood's dancing hoof,
By scummed, starfish sands
With their fishwife cross
Gulls, pipers, cockles, and sails,
Out there, crow black, men
Tackled with clouds, who kneel
To the sunset nets,
Geese nearly in heaven, boys
Stabbing, and herons, and shells
That speak seven seas,
Eternal waters away
From the cities of nine
Days' night whose towers will catch
In the religious wind
Like stalks of tall, dry straw,
At poor peace I sing
To you strangers (though song
Is a burning and crested act,
The fire of birds in
vii

4

Work ark and the moonshine
Drinking Noah of the bay,
With pelt, and scale, and fleece:
Only the drowned deep bells
Of sheep and churches noise
Poor peace as the sun sets
And dark shoals every holy field.
We will ride out alone, and then,
Under the stars of Wales,
Cry, Multitudes of arks!   Across
The water lidded lands,
Manned with their loves they'll move,
Like wooden islands, hill to hill.
Huloo, my prowed dove with a flute!
Ahoy, old, sea-legged fox,
Tom tit and Dai mouse!
My ark sings in the sun
At God speeded summer's end
And the flood flowers now.

5

Author's Prologue

This day winding down now
At God speeded summer's end
In the torrent salmon sun,
In my seashaken house
On a breakneck of rocks
Tangled with chirrup and fruit,
Froth, flute, fin and quill
At a wood's dancing hoof,
By scummed, starfish sands
With their fishwife cross
Gulls, pipers, cockles, and sails,
Out there, crow black, men
Tackled with clouds, who kneel
To the sunset nets,
Geese nearly in heaven, boys
Stabbing, and herons, and shells
That speak seven seas,
Eternal waters away
From the cities of nine
Days' night whose towers will catch
In the religious wind
Like stalks of tall, dry straw,
At poor peace I sing
To you strangers (though song
Is a burning and crested act,
The fire of birds in
vii

6

To Wales in my arms.
Hoo, there, in castle keep,
You king singsong owls, who moonbeam
The flickering runs and dive
The dingle furred deer dead!
Huloo, on plumbed bryns,
O my ruffled ring dove
In the hooting, nearly dark
With Welsh and reverent rook,
Coo rooing the woods' praise,
Who moons her blue notes from her nest
Down to the curlew herd!
Ho, hullaballoing clan
Agape, with woe
In your beaks, on the gabbing capes!
Heigh, on horseback hill, jack
Whisking hare! who
Hears, there, this fox light, my flood ship's
Clangour as I hew and smite
(A clash of anvils for my
Hubbub and fiddle, this tune
On a tongued puffball)
But animals thick as thieves
On God's rough tumbling grounds
(Hail to His beasthood!).
Beasts who sleep good and thin,
Hist, in hogsback woods!   The haystacked
Hollow farms in a throng
Of waters cluck and cling,
And barnroofs cockcrow war!
O kingdom of neighbours, finned
Felled and quilled, flash to my patch
ix

7

Designs for *Swansea version* (above) and *DPDT* (below)

Before I knocked

BEFORE I knocked and flesh let enter,
With liquid hands tapped on the womb,
I who was shapeless as the water
That shaped the Jordan near my home
Was brother to Mnetha's daughter
And sister to the fathering worm.

I who was deaf to spring and summer,
Who knew not sun nor moon by name,
Felt thud beneath my flesh's armour,
As yet was in a molten form,
The leaden stars, the rainy hammer
Swung by my father from his dome.

I knew the message of the winter,
The darted hail, the childish snow,
And the wind was my sister suitor;
Wind in me leaped, the hellborn dew;
My veins flowed with the Eastern weather;
Ungotten I knew night and day.

As yet ungotten, I did suffer;
The rack of dreams my lily bones
Did twist into a living cipher,
And flesh was snipped to cross the lines
Of gallow crosses on the liver
And brambles in the wringing brains

7

8

9

The force that through the green fuse drives the flower

THE force that through the green fuse drives the flower
Drives my green age; that blasts the roots of trees
Is my destroyer.
And I am dumb to tell the crooked rose
My youth is bent by the same wintry fever.

The force that drives the water through the rocks
Drives my red blood; that dries the mouthing streams
Turns mine to wax.
And I am dumb to mouth unto my veins
How at the mountain spring the same mouth sucks.

The hand that whirls the water in the pool
Stirs the quicksand; that ropes the blowing wind
Hauls my shroud sail.
And I am dumb to tell the hanging man
How of my clay is made the hangman's lime.

The lips of time leech to the fountain head;
Love drips and gathers, but the fallen blood
Shall calm her sores.
And I am dumb to tell a weather's wind
How time has ticked a heaven round the stars.

And I am dumb to tell the lover's tomb
How at my sheet goes the same crooked worm.

9

Work ark and the moonshine
Drinking Noah of the bay,
With pelt, and scale, and fleece:
Only the drowned deep bells
Of sheep and churches noise
Poor peace as the sun sets
And dark shoals every holy field.
We will ride out alone, and then,
Under the stars of Wales,
Cry, Multitudes of arks!   Across
The water lidded lands,
Manned with their loves they'll move,
Like wooden islands, hill to hill.
Huloo, my prowed dove with a flute!
Ahoy, old, sea-legged fox,
Tom tit and Dai mouse!
My ark sings in the sun
At God speeded summer's end
And the flood flowers now.

10

11

The force that through the green fuse drives the flower

THE force that through the green fuse drives the flower
Drives my green age; that blasts the roots of trees
Is my destroyer.
And I am dumb to tell the crooked rose
My youth is bent by the same wintry fever.

The force that drives the water through the rocks
Drives my red blood; that dries the mouthing streams
Turns mine to wax.
And I am dumb to mouth unto my veins
How at the mountain spring the same mouth sucks.

The hand that whirls the water in the pool
Stirs the quicksand; that ropes the blowing wind
Hauls my shroud sail.
And I am dumb to tell the hanging man
How of my clay is made the hangman's lime.

The lips of time leech to the fountain head;
Love drips and gathers, but the fallen blood
Shall calm her sores.
And I am dumb to tell a weather's wind
How time has ticked a heaven round the stars.

And I am dumb to tell the lover's tomb
How at my sheet goes the same crooked worm.

9

Designs for *Swansea version* (above) and *DPDT* (below)

Was there a time

WAS there a time when dancers with their fiddles
In children's circuses could stay their troubles?
There was a time they could cry over books,
But time has set its maggot on their track.
Under the arc of the sky they are unsafe.
What's never known is safest in this life.
Under the skysigns they who have no arms
Have cleanest hands, and, as the heartless ghost
Alone's unhurt, so the blind man sees best.

12

Was there a time

WAS there a time when dancers with their fiddles
In children's circuses could stay their troubles?
There was a time they could cry over books,
But time has set its maggot on their track.
Under the arc of the sky they are unsafe.
What's never known is safest in this life.
Under the skysigns they who have no arms
Have cleanest hands, and, as the heartless ghost
Alone's unhurt, so the blind man sees best.

13

O make me a mask

O MAKE me a mask and a wall to shut from your spies
Of the sharp, enamelled eyes and the spectacled claws
Rape and rebellion in the nurseries of my face,
Gag of a dumbstruck tree to block from bare enemies
The bayonet tongue in this undefended prayerpiece,
The present mouth, and the sweetly blown trumpet of lies,
Shaped in old armour and oak the countenance of a dunce
To shield the glistening brain and blunt the examiners,
And a tear-stained widower grief drooped from the lashes
To veil belladonna and let the dry eyes perceive
Others betray the lamenting lies of their losses
By the curve of the nude mouth or the laugh up the sleeve.

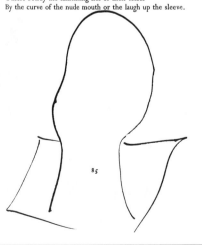

14

O make me a mask

O MAKE me a mask and a wall to shut from your spies
Of the sharp, enamelled eyes and the spectacled claws
Rape and rebellion in the nurseries of my face,
Gag of a dumbstruck tree to block from bare enemies
The bayonet tongue in this undefended prayerpiece,
The present mouth, and the sweetly blown trumpet of lies,
Shaped in old armour and oak the countenance of a dunce
To shield the glistening brain and blunt the examiners,
And a tear-stained widower grief drooped from the lashes
To veil belladonna and let the dry eyes perceive
Others betray the lamenting lies of their losses
By the curve of the nude mouth or the laugh up the sleeve.

15

Designs for *Swansea version* (left) and *DPDT* (right)

This bread I break

This bread I break was once the oat,
This wine upon a foreign tree
Plunged in its fruit;
Man in the day or wind at night
Laid the crops low, broke the grape's joy.

Once in this wind the summer blood
Knocked in the flesh that decked the vine,
Once in this bread
The oat was merry in the wind;
Man broke the sun, pulled the wind down.

This flesh you break, this blood you let
Make desolation in the vein,
Were oat and grape
Born of the sensual root and sap;
My wine you drink, my bread you snap.

16

17

This bread I break

This bread I break was once the oat,
This wine upon a foreign tree
Plunged in its fruit;
Man in the day or wind at night
Laid the crops low, broke the grape's joy.

Once in this wind the summer blood
Knocked in the flesh that decked the vine,
Once in this bread
The oat was merry in the wind;
Man broke the sun, pulled the wind down.

This flesh you break, this blood you let
Make desolation in the vein,
Were oat and grape
Born of the sensual root and sap;
My wine you drink, my bread you snap.

And death shall have no dominion

And death shall have no dominion.
Dead men naked they shall be one
With the man in the wind and the west moon;
When their bones are picked clean and the clean bones gone,
They shall have stars at elbow and foot;
Though they go mad they shall be sane,
Though they sink through the sea they shall rise again;
Though lovers be lost love shall not;
And death shall have no dominion.

And death shall have no dominion.
Under the windings of the sea
They lying long shall not die windily;
Twisting on racks when sinews give way,
Strapped to a wheel, yet they shall not break;
Faith in their hands shall snap in two,
And the unicorn evils run them through;
Split all ends up they shan't crack;
And death shall have no dominion.

And death shall have no dominion.
No more may gulls cry at their ears
Or waves break loud on the seashores;
Where blew a flower may a flower no more
Lift its head to the blows of the rain;
Though they be mad and dead as nails,
Heads of the characters hammer through daisies;
Break in the sun till the sun breaks down,
And death shall have no dominion.

18

19

And death shall have no dominion

And death shall have no dominion.
Dead men naked they shall be one
With the man in the wind and the west moon;
When their bones are picked clean and the clean bones gone,
They shall have stars at elbow and foot;
Though they go mad they shall be sane,
Though they sink through the sea they shall rise again;
Though lovers be lost love shall not;
And death shall have no dominion.

And death shall have no dominion.
Under the windings of the sea
They lying long shall not die windily;
Twisting on racks when sinews give way,
Strapped to a wheel, yet they shall not break;
Faith in their hands shall snap in two,
And the unicorn evils run them through;
Split all ends up they shan't crack;
And death shall have no dominion.

And death shall have no dominion.
No more may gulls cry at their ears
Or waves break loud on the seashores;
Where blew a flower may a flower no more
Lift its head to the blows of the rain;
Though they be mad and dead as nails,
Heads of the characters hammer through daisies;
Break in the sun till the sun breaks down,
And death shall have no dominion.

Designs for *Swansea version* (left) and *DPDT* (right)

20   'Spare' back and front cover design

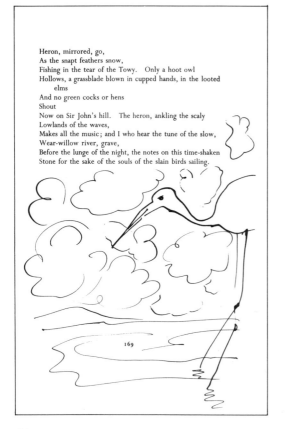

Heron, mirrored, go,
As the snapt feathers snow,
Fishing in the tear of the Towy.   Only a hoot owl
Hollows, a grassblade blown in cupped hands, in the looted
    elms
And no green cocks or hens
Shout
Now on Sir John's hill.   The heron, ankling the scaly
Lowlands of the waves,
Makes all the music; and I who hear the tune of the slow,
Wear-willow river, grave,
Before the lunge of the night, the notes on this time-shaken
Stone for the sake of the souls of the slain birds sailing.

169

COLLECTED POEMS

21   Design for *DPDT*   **22**   Design for half-title page in *Swansea version*

23   *Requiem for Dylan Thomas* (1954). Pen and ink drawing, 15″ x 22″

24

The Hoot Owl (1953). Monoprint in black and white,
13″ x 16″, for the Dylan Thomas Memorial Reading
at the Globe Theatre, London, 1954

25

Homage to Dylan Thomas (1955). Lithograph in
black and white, 16″ x 22″

Do not go gentle into that good night (1955), Oil on canvas, 39$^{1/2}''$ x 17$''$

Do not go gentle into that good night (1965). Lithograph in black and white, $32^{1}/_{4}''$ x $23^{3}/_{8}''$

Here in this spring

HERE in this spring, stars float along the void;
Here in this ornamental winter
Down pelts the naked weather;
This summer buries a spring bird.

Symbols are selected from the years'
Slow rounding of four seasons' coasts,
In autumn teach three seasons' fires
And four birds' notes.

I should tell summer from the trees, the worms
Tell, if at all, the winter's storms
Or the funeral of the sun;
I should learn spring by the cuckooing,
And the slug should teach me destruction.

A worm tells summer better than the clock,
The slug's a living calendar of days;
What shall it tell me if a timeless insect
Says the world wears away?

28

29

Nor that riding to sleep
I should hear him fly with the high fields
And wake to the farm forever fled from the childless land.
Oh as I was young and easy in the mercy of his means,
Time held me green and dying
Though I sang in my chains like the sea.

On no work of words

ON NO work of words now for three lean months in the
  bloody
Belly of the rich year and the big purse of my body
I bitterly take to task my poverty and craft:

To take to give is all, return what is hungrily given
Puffing the pounds of manna up through the dew to heaven,
The lovely gift of the gab bangs back on a blind shaft.

To lift to leave from the treasures of man is pleasing death
That will rake at last all currencies of the marked breath
And count the taken, forsaken mysteries in a bad dark.

To surrender now is to pay the expensive ogre twice.
Ancient woods of my blood, dash down to the nut of the seas
If I take to burn or return this world which is each man's
  work.

30

31

Comes designed to my love to steal not her tide raking
Wound, nor her riding high, nor her eyes, nor kindled hair,
But her faith that each vast night and the saga of prayer
                              He comes to take
Her faith that this last night for his unsacred sake
He comes to leave her in the lawless sun awaking

Naked and forsaken to grieve he will not come.
Ever and ever by all your vows believe and fear
My dear this night he comes and night without end my dear
                              Since you were born:
And you shall wake, from country sleep, this dawn and each
    first dawn,
Your faith as deathless as the outcry of the ruled sun.

Designs from *DPDT*

Twenty-four years

TWENTY-FOUR years remind the tears of my eyes.
(Bury the dead for fear that they walk to the grave in labour.)
In the groin of the natural doorway I crouched like a tailor
Sewing a shroud for a journey
By the light of the meat-eating sun.
Dressed to die, the sensual strut begun,
With my red veins full of money,
In the final direction of the elementary town
I advance for as long as forever is.

32

33

These were the woods the river and sea
Where a boy
In the listening
Summertime of the dead whispered the truth of his joy
To the trees and the stones and the fish in the tide.
And the mystery
Sang alive
Still in the water and singingbirds.

And there could I marvel my birthday
Away but the weather turned around.   And the true
Joy of the long dead child sang burning
In the sun.
It was my thirtieth
Year to heaven stood there then in the summer noon
Though the town below lay leaved with October blood.
O may my heart's truth
Still be sung
On this high hill in a year's turning.

34

35

One enemy, of many, who knows well
Your heart is luminous
In the watched dark, quivering through locks and caves,
Will pull the thunderbolts
To shut the sun, plunge, mount your darkened keys
And sear just riders back,
Until that one loved least
Looms the last Samson of your zodiac.

I turn the corner of prayer and burn
In a blessing of the sudden
Sun. In the name of the damned
I would turn back and run
To the hidden land
But the loud sun
Christens down
The sky.
I
Am found.
O let him
Scald me and drown
Me in his world's wound.
His lightning answers my
Cry. My voice burns in his hand.
Now I am lost in the blinding
One. The sun roars at the prayer's end.

Sun designs from *DPDT*

36 *Mandala* (*Study for 'Afal du Brogŵyr'*) (1952). Watercolour and chalk on wood, 15″ x 22″. (Presented to C. G. Jung.)

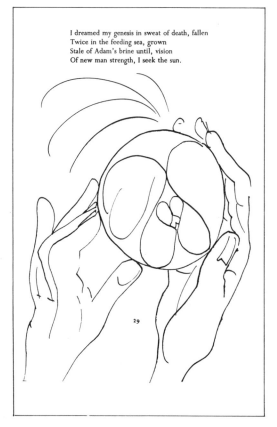

I dreamed my genesis in sweat of death, fallen
Twice in the feeding sea, grown
Stale of Adam's brine until, vision
Of new man strength, I seek the sun.

29

37 'I dreamed my genesis', *Swansea version*

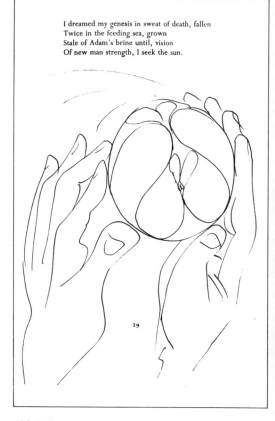

I dreamed my genesis in sweat of death, fallen
Twice in the feeding sea, grown
Stale of Adam's brine until, vision
Of new man strength, I seek the sun.

29

38 'I dreamed my genesis', *Mrs. Thomas's version*

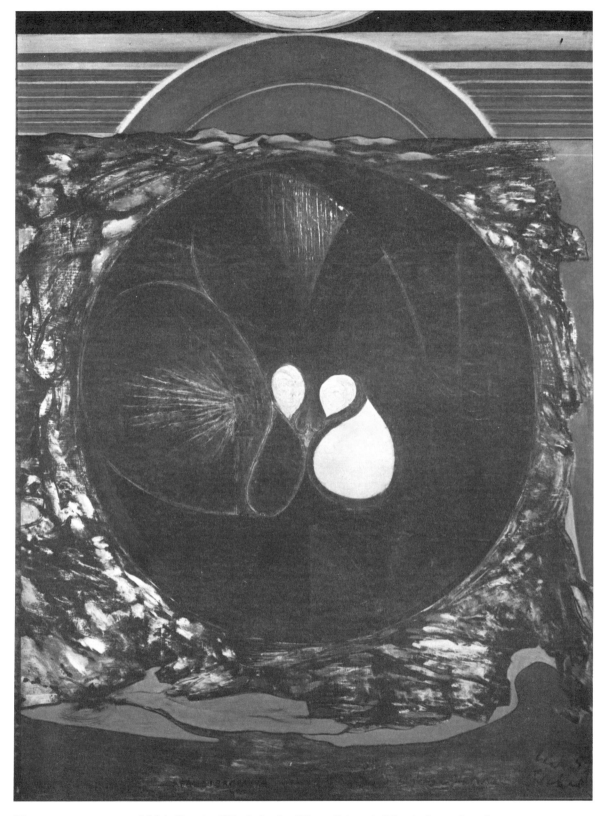

39   *Afal du Brogŵyr* ('Black Apple of Gower') (1952). Oil painting, 40″ x 30″

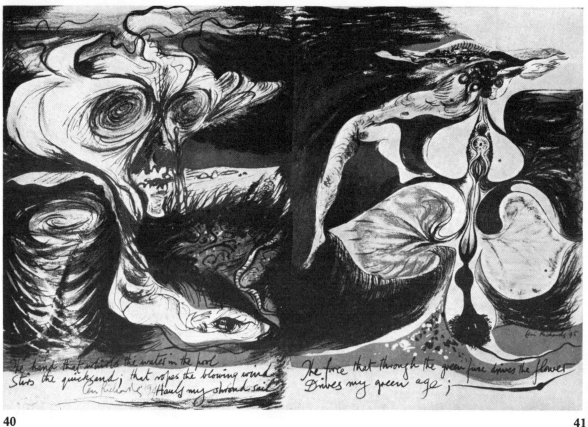

He hand thatwhirls the water in the pool
Stirs the quicksand; that ropes the blowing wind
Len Richards 94Hauls my shroud sail

The force that through the green fuse drives the flower
Drives my green age;

The force that through the green fuse drives the flower
Drives my green age; that blasts the roots of trees
Is my destroyer.
And I am dumb to tell the crooked rose
My youth is bent by the same wintry fever.
The force that drives the water through the rocks
Drives my red blood; that dries the mouthing streams
Turns mine to wax.
And I am dumb to mouth unto my veins
How at the mountain spring the same mouth sucks.

The hand that whirls the water in the pool
Stirs the quicksand; that ropes the blowing wind
Hauls my shroud sail.
And I am dumb to tell the hanging man
How of my clay is made the hangman's lime.

The lips of time leech to the fountain head
Love drips and gathers, but the fallen blood
Shall calm her sores.
And I am dumb to tell a weather's wind
How time has ticked a heaven round the stars.

And I am dumb to tell the lover's tomb
How at my sheet goes the same crooked worm

Dylan Thomas

The force that through the green fuse drives the flower (1945).   Colour lithographs from *Poetry London*

43
The Female Contains All Qualities (1937).
Oil on canvas, 42″ x 35″

44
Two Females (1947).
Monochrome lithograph, 22″

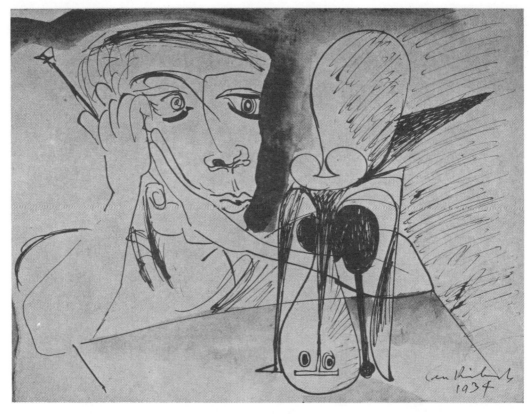

45   *The Sculptor and His Object* (1934). Pen and ink drawing, 11″ x 15¼″

46   *Origin of Species* (1971). Colour screenprint, 25½″ x 31¾″

Notes

A RETROSPECTIVE INTRODUCTION

1   Dylan Thomas, *Collected Poems* 1934-1952, J. M. Dent, London, 1952; referred to in these notes as *CP*.

2   *Some Poems by Richard Burns, Illuminated and Lettered by Frances Richards*, Enitharmon Press, London, 1977.

3   Ceri Richards. *Drawings to Poems by Dylan Thomas*, Enitharmon Press, London, 1980; referred to as *DPDT*.

4   Roberto Sanesi, *The Graphic Works of Ceri Richards*, tr. Richard Burns, Gino Cerastico, Milan, 1973, p.87; referred to in these notes as *GWCR*.

5   It is certain that this book is of enormous importance for a complete understanding of Ceri Richards's work, particularly with regard to his involvement with Dylan Thomas's poems. A plea must be made here to anyone finding it to pass on information of its whereabouts to the publisher of this edition.

6   C. G. Jung, *Letters* (vol.2, 1951-1961), ed. Gerhard Adler, tr. R. F. C. Hull, Routledge & Kegan Paul, London, 1976, pp.440-1.

7   These 'coincidences and correspondences' are discussed in Chapter II of this monograph. Jung called meaningful coincidence 'synchronicity'. He investigated the phenomenon in depth, and proposed a theory about it, many aspects of which tally well with Richards's composition of the *DPDT* series on the eve of Thomas's death, the patterns of symbolism in the drawings themselves, and certain other factors. The following statement by Jung in his essay 'Synchronicity: An Acausal Connecting Principle' gives some indication of the relevance of his insights and arguments: "Synchronicity . . . consists of two factors: a) an unconscious image comes into consciousness either directly (i.e. literally) or indirectly (symbolised or suggested) in the form of a dream, idea or premonition. b) An objective situation coincides with this content." See C. G. Jung and W. Pauli, *The Interpretation of Nature and*

the Psyche, tr. R. F. C. Hull, Routledge & Kegan Paul, London, 1955, p.44. The essay is reprinted in C. G. Jung, *The Structure and Dynamics of the Psyche* (Collected Works, vol.8), Routledge & Kegan Paul, London, 1960. For further application of the theory, see also Jung's foreword to *The I Ching or Book of Changes*, tr. Richard Wilhelm, Routledge & Kegan Paul, London, 1951, particularly pp.xxiv-xxv.

8   C. G. Jung, *Memories, Dreams, Reflections*, tr. Richard and Clara Winston, Collins and Routledge & Kegan Paul, London, 1963. See in particular pp.136, 188-9 and 281-3; and also the concluding section of this monograph.

9   Quoted by Sanesi in *GWCR*, p.6.

10 See Walter Perrie's preface to his long poem *By Moon and Sun*, Canongate, Edinburgh, 1980, particularly pp.ix-x. His comments on both causality and symbolism in that essay also have bearings on Jung's synchronicity theory. See also the essay on symbolism in W. Perrie, *Out of Conflict*, Borderline Press, Dunfermline, forthcoming, 1982.

11 See C. G. Jung, *Memories, Dreams, Reflections*, p.184.

12 Jean Markale, *Women of the Celts*, tr. Heather Cremonesi, Gordon & Cremonesi, London, 1975.

13 See note 7 above.

14 See in particular Erich Neumann, *The Great Mother*, tr. Ralph Manheim, Bollingen Series XLVII, Princeton University Press, 1955; and *Art and the Creative Unconscious*, Bollingen Series LXI, Princeton University Press, 1959.

15 See 'Psychology and Literature' and 'On the Relation of Analytical Psychology to the Poetic Art' in C. G. Jung, *The Spirit in Man, Art, and Literature* (Collected Works, vol.15), Routledge & Kegan Paul, London, 1966; and 'Art and Time' and 'Creative Man and Transformation' in E. Neumann, op.cit., 1959.

Chapter I.

THOMAS AND RICHARDS : PATTERNS OF INFLUENCE

1   Roberto Sanesi, introductory essay to *GWCR*, p.9.

2   Sanesi, *GWCR*, pp.7-8.

3   In *Homage to Ceri Richards*, Fischer Fine Art catalogue, London, 1972.

4   Sanesi, *GWCR*, p.10.

5 Roberto Sanesi, *Nella coscia del gigante bianco*, La Nuova Foglio, Macerata, 1975, p.28.

6 *CP*, p.13.

7 See *GWCR*, pp.87-103, for reproductions and commentary, and particularly pp.88 and 89 for the use of quotations from poems in visual designs.

8 Sanesi, *GWCR*, p.87.

9 Sanesi, *GWCR*, p.87.

10 Henry Vaughan, 'The Retreate', in *Poetry and Selected Prose*, ed. L. C. Martin, Oxford University Press, 1963, p.249.

11 E. Neumann, op.cit., 1959, pp.201-2.

Chapter II

COINCIDENCES AND CORRESPONDENCES

1 *GWCR*, p.87.

2 See figs. 1, 3, 30 and 32, and also *DPDT*, p.138.

3 E. Neumann, op.cit., 1959, pp.94-5 and 131.

4 *CP*, p.179.

5 *CP*, p.173.

6 *CP* and *DPDT*, p.161, and see fig. 29.

7 *CP*, p.174.

8 *CP*, pp.152 and 157.

9 See front cover of this book and figs. 1, 2, 21, 30, 32 and 33; and *DPDT*, title-page, dedication page and pp.44 and 169.

10 For some of Richards's works in the series *La Cathédrale Engloutie*, see *GWCR*, pp.75-79, and pp.13-14 of the introduction for background and commentary.

11 *CP*, pp.150 and 152.

12 *CP*, p.131.

13 *The Mabinogion*, tr. Gwyn Jones and Thomas Jones, Everyman edition, J. M. Dent, London, 1973, pp.63-4.

14 *CP*, p.56.

15 *CP*, p.135.

16 *CP* and *DPDT*, p.166, and see fig. 31.

17 *CP*, p.178.

18 *CP* and *DPDT*, pp.138 and 148, and see fig. 35.

19 *CP*, p.171.

20 *CP*, p.66.

21 *CP* and *DPDT*, p.116.

22 See *CP* and DPDT, in *Note* following dedication page.

23 Quoted by Constantine Fitzgibbon, *The Life of Dylan Thomas*, J. M. Dent, London, 1975 edition, p.161.

24 See *The Oxford Book of English Verse*, ed. Sir Arthur Quiller-Couch, Oxford University Press, 1957 edition, p.541.

25 Rainer Maria Rilke, *Duino Elegies*, tr. J. B. Leishman and Stephen Spender, Hogarth Press, London, 1939, p.25.

26 Reproduced in *GWCR*, p.99.

27 See also *GWCR*, for *Homage to Dylan Thomas*, a black and white lithograph, 1955.

28 Reproduced in *GWCR*, pp.90-95.

29 See note 7 in Chapter I for Jung's theory of synchronicity, which is relevant to our discussion of the skull-imagery in these drawings, in the context of the date of Dylan Thomas's death one day after they were composed.

30 Arnold van Gennep, *The Rites of Passage*, Chicago, 1961.

31 E. Neumann, op.cit., 1959, pp.121-2.

Chapter III

FORM AND CONTENT IN THE DRAWINGS

1 In the catalogue for Roberto Sanesi's poem *Journey Toward the North (Viaggio verso il nord)*, illustrated by Ceri Richards, Collana 'Gli Smeraldi' no.9, Gino Cerastico, Milan, 1973. For reproductions of some of Richards's illustrations, see *GWCR*, pp.131-140.

2 In *Journey Toward the North*, op.cit., 1973.

3   Quoted in an essay 'Art and Objective Truth' by George Lukacs in his *Writer and Critic*, tr. Arthur Kahn, Merlin Press, London, 1970, p.45.

4   See Eugene Herrigel, *Zen in the Art of Archery*, tr. R. F. C. Hull, Routledge & Kegan Paul, London, 1953.

5   For example, see *DPDT*, pp.23 and 81.

6   See figs. 1 and 3, and also *DPDT*, pp.3, 6 and 127.

7   For example, see *DPDT*, pp.62 and 147.

8   *DPDT*, p.146.

9   William Blake, 'The Vision of the Last Judgement'. See Blake, *Poetry and Prose*, ed. Geoffrey Keynes, Nonesuch Library, London, 1956 edition, p.652.

10 For discussion of the symbolism of the circle in modern art, see Aniela Jaffé, 'Symbolism in the Visual Arts' in *Man and His Symbols*, ed. C. G. Jung, Aldus Books, London, 1964, pp.247-249.

11 *CP* and *DPDT*, p.128.

12 P. B. Shelley, in *Poetical Works*, ed. Thomas Hutchinson, Oxford University Press, 1919, pp.573-4.

13 George Herbert, *Poems*, ed. Helen Gardner, Oxford University Press, 1961, pp.78 and 85.

14 Boris Pasternak, *Dr. Zhivago*, tr. Max Hayward and Manya Harari, Fontana edition, London, 1970, pp.480-1.

15 See for example figs. 1, 3, 17, 19, 21, 28-32, and also figs. 20 and 22.

16 For discussion of the *Shekhinah*, see the works of Gershom Scholem, especially *Major Trends in Jewish Mysticism*, Routledge & Kegan Paul, London, 1955.

17 *CP* and *DPDT*, p.164.

Chapter IV

VARIANTS OF THE DRAWINGS

1   See note 5, to Chapter I.

2   See inside back cover of *DPDT*. This drawing originally appeared on p.178 of *CP*, beneath the poem 'In the white giant's thigh', though it is not especially related to the content of that poem.

3   *CP* and *DPDT*, pp.168-9.

4   *CP*, pp.170 and 172.

5   *CP* and *DPDT*, p.102.

6   J. Markale, op.cit., pp.72-3.

7   'Capturing Animals': originally a BBC *Poetry for Schools* broadcast, and available as a BBC record. Published in Ted Hughes, *Poetry in the Making*, Faber & Faber, London, 1967. See pp.17, 19 and 21.

8   J. E. Cirlot, *A Dictionary of Symbols*, tr. Jack Sage, Routledge & Kegan Paul, London, 1971, p.108.

9   I am indebted to Kim Landers for pointing out to me that there is more than a hint of the traditional baby-bearing stork in the bird which I have identified as a heron in this drawing, particularly through the association of basket or cradle with the upturned skull which the bird holds in its beak. The visual pun suggested by this interpretation fits neatly with our argument that the upturned skull symbolises new life, joy, and hope, and even more so, with Richards's use of lines from Thomas's 'Poem on his birthday' in the drawing.

10   J. Markale, op.cit., pp.173-200.

11   *CP*, p.173.

12   See *GWCR*, pp.89 and 99 for reproductions.

13   These are *DPDT*, pp. ix, 6, 88, 99, 108, 112, 118, 128, 146 and 166. The best of these, I believe, are those on pp. 99, 118, 128 and 186 (see figs. 32, 34, 3 and 31 respectively), and also the tramp on p.112.

14   These are *CP* and Swansea version, pp.7, 141 and 142, and the half-title page.

15   For Thomas's outline of this unfinished long poem, see the introduction to his radio talk, 'Three Poems' in *Quite Early One Morning*, J. M. Dent, London, 1954, pp.155-7.

16   Reprinted in Roberto Sanesi, *Ceri Richards, Rilievi, disegni e dipinti*, 1933/1940, La Nuova Foglio, Macerata, 1976.

17   See particularly C. G. Jung, *Symbols of Transformation* (Collected Works, vol.5), Routledge & Kegan Paul, London, 1956.

18   See note 7, to Chapter I. The following statement by Jung in his foreword to the *I Ching* (op.cit., pp.xxiv-xxv) is also relevant to Richards's comment about "matching the pace of time to an intuitive change."
       The ancient Chinese mind contemplates the cosmos in a way comparable to that of the modern physicist, who cannot deny that his model

of the world is a decidedly psychophysical structure. The microphysical event includes the observer just as much as the reality underlying the *I Ching* comprises subjective, i.e. psychic conditions in the totality of the momentary situation. Just as causality describes the sequence of events, so synchronicity to the Chinese mind deals with the coincidence of events. The causal point of view tells us a dramatic story about how *D* came into existence: it took its origin from *C*, which existed before *D*, and *C* in its turn had a father, *B*, etc. The synchronistic view on the other hand tries to produce an equally meaningful picture of coincidence. How does it happen that *A'*, *B'*, *C'*, *D'*, etc, appear all in the same moment and in the same place? It happens in the first place because the physical events *A'* and *B'* are of the same quality as the psychic events *C'* and *D'*, and further because all are the exponents of one and the same momentary situation. The situation is assumed to represent a legible or understandable picture.

19   Quoted by C. Fitzgibbon, op.cit., p.241.

Chapter V

THE 'BLACK APPLE OF GOWER' AND ITS SYMBOLISM

1   C. G. Jung, *Letters*, vol.2, p.440.

2   Henry Vaughan, 'They are all gone into the world of light', op.cit., p.318.

3   Heracleitus, *On the Universe*, ed. W. H. S. Jones, Loeb Classical Library, No. 150, London, 1967 edition, p.493.

4   William Wordsworth, *The Prelude*, Book II, lines 403-5 (1805 text), ed. Ernest de Selincourt, Oxford University Press, 1969 edition, p.31.

5   C. G. Jung, *Collected Works*, vol.15, op.cit., pp.82-3.

6   John Donne, 'A Better Resurrection', in *Poetry and Prose*, ed. H. W. Garrod, Oxford University Press, 1957, pp.96-100.

7   *CP* and *DPDT*, p.9, and see also figs. 9 and 11.

8   *CP* and *DPDT*, p.99.

9   W. B. Yeats, *Collected Poems*, Macmillan, London, 1961, p.281.

10   Alfred Lord Tennyson, in *The Oxford Book of English Verse*, op.cit., p.857.

11   *CP* and *DPDT*, p.28.

12   *CP*, p.131.

13 Quoted by C. Fitzgibbon, op.cit., p.163.

14 *CP*, p.136.

15 C. G. Jung, *Alchemical Studies* (Collected Works, vol.13), Routledge & Kegan Paul, London, 1967, note to p.266.

16 J. E. Cirlot, op.cit., p.320.

17 *CP* and *DPDT*, p.160.

18 J. Markale, op.cit., pp.240-1.

19 J. E. Cirlot, op.cit., p.152.

20 J. E. Cirlot, op.cit., pp.319 and 320.

21 Helmut Wilhelm, *Change, Eight Lectures on the 'I Ching'*, tr. Cary F. Baynes, Routledge & Kegan Paul, London, 1975 edition, p.39.

22 C. G. Jung, *Symbols of Transformation* (Collected Works, vol.5), Routledge & Kegan Paul, London, 1956, pp.209-10.

23 C. G. Jung, *Collected Works*, vol.5, op.cit., p.207.

24 The Revelation of St. John, Chapter 21, verse 1, *The Bible*, Authorised Version.

25 *CP*, p.51.

26 See Eliot Elisofon and Alan Watts. *The Temple of Konarak: Erotic Spirituality*, Thames & Hudson, London, 1971, p.11.

27 Robert Melville, catalogue introduction for the Marlborough Gallery's retrospective exhibition of Ceri Richards's work, London, 1965.

28 E. Elisofon and A. Watts, op.cit., pp.89-90.

29 W. B. Yeats, op.cit., pp.66-7.

30 *CP*, p.130.

31 Merlin Stone, *The Paradise Papers : The Suppression of Women's Rites*, Virago, London, 1979, pp.238-9.

32 In the Fitzwilliam Museum, Cambridge.

33 See E. Neumann, op.cit., 1955, pp.126, 244, 255 and 276, and his plate 35.

34 The relevance of these works to the images of Thomas and Richards has been developed in detail by Roberto Sanesi in his juxtaposition of illustrations in *Nella coscia del gigante bianco*, q.v.

35 In Octavio Paz, *Configurations*, Jonathan Cape, London, 1971.

36 *CP*, *p*.51.

37 *CP* and *DPDT*, p.127.

38 J. Markale, op.cit., pp.79-80.

39 J. Markale, op.cit., pp.80-81.

40 J. Markale, op.cit., pp.239-40.

41 J. Markale, op.cit., pp.154-5.

42 I am indebted to John Paul Dick for pointing out the hidden owl in this work, and also for reminding me that Max Ernst liked owls.

43 *CP* and *DPDT*, p.ix.

44 E. Neumann, op.cit., 1955, p.180.

45 E. Neumann, op.cit., 1955, p.278.

46 J. E. Cirlot, op.cit., p.247.

47 Alan Garner, *The Owl Service*, Fontana Books, London, 1973.

48 J. Markale, op.cit., p.149.

49 *The Mabinogion*, op.cit., pp.73-4.

50 J. Markale, op.cit., p.150-3.

51 J. Markale, op.cit., p.151.

52 J. Markale, op.cit., p.151.

53 I am indebted to Kim Landers for reminding me of the virginal attributes of Arianrod, which discredit a simple Freudian interpretation of the myth.

54 C. G. Jung, *Collected Works*, vol.5, op.cit., p.223.

55 See M. Stone, op.cit., for related discussion on the position of women in Christian writings.

56 J. Markale, op.cit., p.153.

57 See *GWCR*, pp.84-5, for commentary and reproduction, and also pp.110-11, which reproduces Vernon Watkin's 'Elegaic Sonnet' (written in memory of Dylan Thomas), and Ceri Richards's lithographs for that poem.

58 Alan Garner, op.cit., p.156.

59 R. Melville, op.cit., 1965.

60 *GWCR*, p.6.

61   W. Blake, op.cit., p.75.

62   M. Stone, op.cit., pp.231-4.

63   *CP* and *DPDT*, p.116.

64   C. G. Jung, *Septem Sermones ad Mortuos*, tr. H. G. Baynes, Stuart & Watkins, London, 1967.

65   C. G. Jung, *Memories, Dreams, Reflections*, op.cit., p.183.

66   C. G. Jung, *Memories, Dreams, Reflections*, op.cit., p.184.

67   C. G. Jung, *Septem Sermones ad Mortuos*, pp.18-22.

68   E. Neumann, op.cit., 1955, p.xlii.

Bibliography

A. SOURCES, AND BIOGRAPHICAL AND CRITICAL REFERENCES ON RICHARDS AND THOMAS

Constantine Fitzgibbon, *The Life of Dylan Thomas*, J. M. Dent, London, 1975.

Homage to Ceri Richards 1903-1971, Fischer Fine Art catalogue, London, 1972.

C. G. Jung, *Letters* 1951-1961 (vol.2), ed. Gerhard Adler, tr. R. F. C. Hull, Routledge & Kegan Paul, London, 1976.

Ceri Richards, *Catalogue* for retrospective exhibition at the Marlborough Gallery with an introduction by Robert Melville, London, 1965.

Ceri Richards, *The Graphic Works*, ed. with an introduction by Roberto Sanesi, tr. Richard Burns, Gino Cerastico, Milan, 1973; abbreviated as *GWCR*.

Ceri Richards, *Rilievi, disegni e dipinti*, 1931/1940, ed. with an introduction by Roberto Sanesi, tr. Rodney Stringer, La Nuova Foglio, Macerata, 1976.

Ceri Richards, *Drawings to Poems by Dylan Thomas*, with an introduction by Richard Burns, Enitharmon Press, London, 1980; abbreviated as *DPDT*.

Ceri Richards and Roberto Sanesi, *Journey Towards the North*, Collana 'Gli Smeraldi' No. 9, Gino Cerastico, Milan, 1973.

Roberto Sanesi, *Nella coscia del gigante bianco*, La Nuova Foglio, Macerata, 1975.

Dylan Thomas, *Collected Poems 1934-1952*, J. M. Dent, London, 1952, abbreviated as *CP*.

Dylan Thomas, *Quite Early One Morning*, J. M. Dent, London, 1954.

B. OTHER

The Bible, Authorised Version.

William Blake, *Poetry and Prose*, ed. Geoffrey Keynes, Nonesuch Library, London, 1956.

Richard Burns, *Some Poems, Illuminated by Frances Richards*, Enitharmon Press, London, 1977.

J. E. Cirlot, *A Dictionary of Symbols*, tr. Jack Sage, Routledge & Kegan Paul, London, 1971.

John Donne, *Poetry and Prose*, ed. H. W. Garrod, Oxford University Press, 1957.

Eliot Elisofon and Alan Watts, *The Temple of Konarak: Erotic Spirituality*, Thames & Hudson, London, 1971.

Alan Garner, *The Owl Service*, Fontana Books, London, 1973.

Heracleitus, *On the Universe*, ed. W. H. S. Jones, Loeb Classical Library, No. 150, London, 1967.

George Herbert, *Poems*, ed. Helen Gardner, Oxford University Press, 1961.

Eugene Herrigel, *Zen in the Art of Archery*, tr. R. F. C. Hull, Routledge & Kegan Paul, London, 1953.

Ted Hughes, *Poetry in the Making*, Faber & Faber, London, 1967.

The I Ching, or Book of Changes, tr. Richard Wilhelm, with a foreword by C. G. Jung, Routledge & Kegan Paul, London, 1951.

Aniela Jaffé, 'Symbolism in the Visual Arts' in *Man and His Symbols*, ed. C. G. Jung, Aldus Books, London, 1964.

C. G. Jung, *Symbols of Transformation* (Collected Works, vol.5, 1956), *The Structure and Dynamics of the Psyche* (Collected Works, vol.8, 1960); *Alchemical Studies* (Collected Works, vol.13, 1967); *The Spirit in Man, Art and Literature* (Collected Works, vol.15, 1966); all tr. R. F. C. Hull, Routledge & Kegan Paul, London.

C. G. Jung, *Memories, Dreams, Reflections*, tr. Richard & Clara Winston, Collins and Routledge & Kegan Paul, London, 1963.

C. G. Jung, *Septem Sermones ad Mortuos*, tr. H. G. Baynes, Stuart & Watkins, London, 1967.

C. G. Jung and W. Pauli, *The Interpretation of Nature and the Psyche*, tr. R. F. C. Hull, Routledge & Kegan Paul, London, 1955.

John Keats, in *The Oxford Book of English Verse*.

Georg Lukacs, *Writer and Critic*, tr. Arthur Kahn, Merlin Press, London, 1970.

The Mabinogion, tr. Gwyn Jones and Thomas Jones, Everyman Library, J. M. Dent, London, 1973.

Jean Markale, *Women of the Celts*, Gordon & Cremonesi, tr. Heather Cremonesi, London, 1975.

Erich Neumann, *The Great Mother* (Bollingen Series XLVIII, 1955) and *Art and the Creative Unconscious* (Bollingen Series LXI, 1959), tr. Ralph Manheim, Princeton University Press.

The Oxford Book of English Verse, ed. Sir Arther Quiller-Couch, Oxford University Press, 1957 edition.

Boris Pasternak, *Dr. Zhivago*, tr. Max Hayward and Manya Harari, Fontana Books, London, 1970.

Octavio Paz, *Configurations*, Jonathan Cape, London, 1971.

Walter Perrie, *By Moon and Sun*, Canongate, Edinburgh, 1980, and *Out of Conflict*, Borderline Press, Dunfermline, 1982.

Rainer Maria Rilke, *Duino Elegies*, tr. J. B. Leishman and Stephen Spender, Hogarth Press, London, 1939.

Gershom Scholem, *Major Trends in Jewish Mysticism*, Routledge & Kegan Paul, London, 1955.

P. B. Shelley, *Poetical Works*, ed. Thomas Hutchinson, Oxford University Press, 1919; and *A Defence of Poetry*.

Merlin Stone, *The Paradise Papers: The Suppression of Women's Rites*, Virago, London, 1979.

Alfred Lord Tennyson, in *The Oxford Book of English Verse*.

Arnold van Gennep, *Rites of Passage*, Chicago, 1961.

Henry Vaughan, *Poetry and Selected Prose*, ed. L. C. Martin, Oxford University Press, 1963.

Helmut Wilhelm, *Change, Eight Lectures on the 'I Ching'*, tr. Cary F. Baynes, Routledge & Kegan Paul, London, 1961.

William Wordsworth, *The Prelude*, 1805 text, ed. Ernest de Selincourt, Oxford University Press, 1969.

W. B. Yeats, *Collected Poems*, Macmillan, London, 1960.